INTERNATIONAL LAW

INTERNATIONAL LAW
AND
CUSTOM
IN ANCIENT INDIA

PRAMATHANATH BANDYOPADHYAY

GYAN

Published by

GYAN

Gyan Publishing House
5, Ansari Road
Daryaganj, New Delhi-110002
Phone: 011-47034999, 9811692060
E-mail: books@gyanbooks.com

Distribution Network
gyanbooks.com
India, USA, Canada, UK, Australia

ISBN: 978-93-7133-292-7 (PB)

First Published, 1920

2nd Impression 2025

Printed at: Gyan Press, Delhi.

INTERNATIONAL LAW
Arthur PRAMATHANATH BANDYOPADHYAY

INTERNATIONAL LAW AND CUSTOM IN ANCIENT INDIA

INTERNATIONAL LAW

AND

CUSTOM

IN ANCIENT INDIA

By

Pramathanath Bandyopadhyay, M.A., B.L.,

Premchand Roychand Scholar, Onauthnauth Deb Research Scholar in Law; Fellow and Member of the Syndicate, Calcutta University; Lecturer in the Post-Graduate Departments of History and Economics; Professor, University Law College, Calcutta; Member, Asiatic Society, Bengal, etc., etc.

CALCUTTA UNIVERSITY PRESS

1920

CONTENTS.

International Law and Custom in Ancient India

INTRODUCTION

Eminent jurists and disinterested publicists regard International Law as the product of modern European culture. They do not deny that the ancients—by the ancients they mean exclusively the Greeks and the Romans—had a distinctive civilisation of their own; but obsessed with the Austinian conception of law they refuse to believe that the constitution of ancient societies was at all favourable for the development of a body of systematic rules. Sir F. E. Smith, the Attorney-General of England, in the most recently published book on International Law gives the following testimonial to ancient societies:

"The constitution of ancient societies was little favourable to the development of International Law. Since states are its units, International Law can only exist where a number of communities acknowledge a mutual equality before the law and make common submission to its authority." Such conditions, says the great lawyer, did not prevail amongst the nations of antiquity in general. He rates the ancients—meaning of course the Greeks and the Romans—because certain rules or customs which guided the relations between people of cognate race were not observed with regard to people outside that pale. "For the most part a state of hostility characterized the relationships between a nation and alien races. Might was regarded as right. Neither person, nor property was considered sacred."[1]

Kent,[2] in his Commentary on International Law held the same view. Even the most civilized states amongst the ancients, according to him, had no conception of the moral obligations of humanity and justice between nations, and that no such thing as International Law obtained among them. Wheaton[3] was no less disparaging in his opinion concerning International Law in Greece. "In the ancient world," says he, "the law of might was universal......that even Aristides the Just was guided by state-interest rather than by justice." According to Oppenheim,[4] the ancients could not possibly have any regard for man as man, or for territorial rights; the stranger was regarded by them as a spy and the normal condition of things was war, during which everything was permissible.

In the "well-considered" opinions of the above jurists therefore, very little of a systematic body of rules governing interstatal relationships could be looked for in antiquity, even among the Greeks and the Romans who have admittedly bequeathed a rich legacy of culture to the modern European nations. International Law therefore, has until quite recently, been regarded as a tardy offshoot of modern civilisation. Imbued with imperialistic ideas, Hall[5] considers International Law as a 'favoured monopoly' of the European family of nations and he regards with great complacence and philosophic satisfaction, "the tendency which has shown itself of late to conduct relations with states, which are outside the sphere of International Law, to a certain extent in accordance with its rules." "A tendency has also shown itself on the part of such states to expect that European

---

[1] F. E. Smith: International Law, p. 1. [2] P. 11.
[3] Introduction. [4] International Law, I. § 37. [5] International Law, p. 40.

countries shall behave in conformity with the standard which they have themselves set up."

Hall was obviously referring to the cases of China and Japan. The case of India, stood on a different footing as she was neither a sovereign state, nor a "civilised" state. Such a considerate publicist like Lawrence[1] would regard the Indian troops as "semi-civilised or imperfectly civilised troops" and he recommended their "use against border tribes and in warfare with people of the same degree of civilisation as themselves." To such people saturated with the theory of the European origin of International Law, the admission of India in the peace conference this year (1919) was regarded as either an "eye wash," or as the legitimate exercise of the right of "self-determination." The signing of the peace treaty by two Indian agents of the Government of India—not the accredited representatives of the people—was regarded by most Indians "as a parting of the old ways," the herald of a brighter dawn, when the westernised education of the Indians would have a distinct though late recognition by the civilised nations of the world. To them India was a

> "..............Sad relic of departed worth,
> Immortal, though no more, though fallen, great"

It is, however, the object of the present thesis to establish the apparently incredible fact that *the ancient Indians had a definite knowledge of the rules of International Law according to which they regulated their international conduct.* Warfare was conducted according to such customs and usages, and the rule of might and the doctrine of state-necessity had no more elaborate applications with them as with the 'moderners,' in their cynical disregard of the rights of others as has been evidenced during the last great world war, in the violation of Luxemburg, and Belgium, in the compulsory enlistment of Greece,

[1] Lawrence: International Law.

after the violation of her neutrality, in the utter disregard for all rules of civilised warfare and in the curtailment of the rights of the non-combatants to the lowest limits. The ancient Indians had two thousand years before a Grotius, a Rachel or an Ayala recalled Europe to humanity, propounded a body of rules governing the relations between different states into which the continent of India was generally divided.

Nor could we, in the face of modern researches, attribute the rules of International Law solely to modern European ingenuity, to modern European thought, to modern European culture and to the powerful writings of European jurists like Grotius, Rachel, Ayala, Puffendorff, Bynkershoeck or Vattel. We have a dim perception of the rudiments of International Law in ancient Egypt. To Mr. Petrie is due the undying gratitude of every orientalist because of his discovery and interpretation of what we now call the Tel-el-amarna and the Boghazköy inscriptions. They clearly prove the international consciousness of ancient Egypt. Intercourse between Egypt and the countries in Syria was maintained by diplomatic agents; hostages were demanded and kept and lastly, the Egyptians entered into elaborate extradition treaties with the Hittites for the protection of their national industries.

Mr. Martin[1] in his "Traces of International Law in China" has pointed out the existence of International Law in China long before the dawn of the Christian era. Diplomatic agents maintained interstatal relationship in China: they were immune from personal violence and the sanction of religion was invoked to mitigate the rigours of Chinese warfare.

Mr. Philipson has clearly established the existence of International Law in ancient Greece. Apart from rules relating to "naturalisation" and "aliens" the Greeks

---

[1] History of Roman Law: Curtis Ed., § 181.

had rules relating to hospitality, asylum, extradition, diplomatic agents and intervention. They firmly grasped the principles of the theory of the Balance of Power and actually used them in practice. They had also rules relating to the declaration and cessation of hostilities, rules relating to the treatment of combatants, to maritime jurisdiction, embargo, blockade and neutrality. Similarly, the Romans had a variety of international rules relating to various topics dealt with by modern International Law; alliances, arbitration, naturalisation, extradition, immunity of ambassadors, procedure and formalities in the conclusion of treaties, right of asylum, treatment of enemy person and enemy property. They had a clear cut conception of protectorates and territorial sovereignty; they knew the position of hostages and the doctrine of *post liminium* owes its origin to them. With the gradual expansion of Rome, all these rules of International Law were frequently violated till the Roman foreign policy was summed up in one word—the triumph of expediency. The foreign policy of the later Roman Republic and the Roman Empire has been admirably described by Ortolan[1] thus:—

"To sow discord among different nations in order to array one against another—to assist the vanquished in conquering the conqueror—to husband its own resources, to use those of its allies to invade the territories of its neighbours—to interfere in the disputes of other states, so as to protect the weaker party and finally to subjugate both—to wage unnecessary wars and prove itself stronger in reverses than in success—to evade oaths and treaties by subterfuge—to practise every kind of injustice under the specious guise of equity—this was the policy which gave Rome the sceptre of all Italy and which was destined to secure for it that of the entire known world."

---

[1] History of Roman Law: Curtis Ed., § 181.

If Europe owes the invention of gunpowder to the Saracens, it owes also its first systematic war code to them. Thus precepts of kindness and chivalry abounded in the Quoran and in the decisions of Mohammad and his successors. There were injunctions against the making use of incendiary projectiles, cutting trees belonging to the enemy, intercepting his water-supply or poisoning wells and water courses, while the killing of women and children or the insane and the mutilation of prisoners without order was absolutely forbidden. Women and minors of both sexes became the immediate property of captors. The disposition of adult male persons was reserved to the commander. They could be sent back, released on ransom, exchanged or reduced to slavery. The giving of food to the prisoners was compulsory, and their torture was prohibited. Captured enemy property became the property of the whole Mussalman community. Booty could not be appropriated till after a fifth had been taken from it for religious purposes. These rules were very frequently violated in actual practice even by the Saracens themselves; but the Turks who succeeded them did not perceive the utility of observing any rules whatsoever in their dealings with non-Mussalmans and betrayed their Turanian origin by habitual disregard of them.

From what has been said above, it would appear that rules of International Law are not exclusively of European origin. The rules of interstatal relationships followed in ancient India were much more humane and much more elaborate than the rules followed by all nations of antiquity and even by nations of modern Europe down perhaps to the time of the French Revolution.

The geographical configuration of India, her early political development and her intellectual expansion all point to the frequency of regularised interstatal relations. Unlike Greece, the various states of India were not isolated from each other. Hills and dales were in plenty in this vast continent of India, but they did not help the development of autonomous city states as in ancient Greece. Although city republics were in existence, they did not form the ideal of political organization in ancient India: on the contrary the country state was the prevailing type of advanced political organisation. The territories of these country states were contiguous to each other and political development as well as commercial intercourse necessitated the observance of a body of rules governing such intercourse. India could not therefore develop what is called in the case of Greece "intermunicipal law." Her geography stood in her way.

The political development of the ancient Indians also helped the growth of interstatal rules. The chief accusation brought against the Indians has been their utter lack of a perfected and lasting imperial organisation. The idea of imperialism had no doubt ruled the minds of men in India in the distant past long before the vista of a vast imperial organisation was opened up to the Indian eye by the invasion of the Persian Emperor Darius or the Macedonian conqueror, Alexander the Great. But the establishment of an empire in India was the exception and not the rule. This lack of an imperial organisation in India, however reproachful to the imperialistic school, was helpful to the establishment of a body of rules guiding the conduct of states in their daily intercourse with the other states, either in times of profound peace or in anxious times of war. Behind this fortuitous concourse of circumstances stood the ever present sanction of religion or *Dharma* which differentiated modern International Law from ancient International Law. Followers of Austin have denied the title International Law to rules based on religious sanction. They put their case too high. All laws are not *laws* according to the positive theory of Austin. Thus Jenks in his "Law and Politics in the Middle Ages" has shown that in mediæval times there existed a body of rules propounded by merchant guilds, by the Church, or based on feudal customs which were laws but could not be regarded as "laws" according to the Austinian sense of the term. If that is the case with municipal law how very different would be the case with International Law? International Law has not ceased to be law because admittedly up to the present day, it has lacked the element of sanction, or coercion in cases of infringement. Rules of International Law have been in the past based on moral persuasion followed by physical compulsion in cases of grave infringements. No common superior has yet enforced the sanction of International Law, though time alone can prove if the "Big Five" in the contemplated League of Nations will be in a position to enforce obedience by making huge sacrifices of accumulated interests, or whether national pride and national prejudices will convert the league into a second Holy Alliance. Prophecy is risky but the contracting units appear restive.

The ancient Hindus did not lack in the idea of the positive sanction of law but they preferred to base the rules relating to interstatal relationship on *Dharma*, or religion as the sheet anchor of common humanity. They had no special code of International Law but as will be seen later, their Dharmasastras and their Arthasastras lay down a body of rules guiding their interstatal relations under the title, *Deshadharma*. A careful study of *Niti* was particularly recommended by the Arthasastras as conducive to all-round prosperity. Thus, belief in the efficacy of a Science of polity as a condition precedent to progress leads to increased intercourse between states on approved lines. Thus says Kautilya :

वृद्धिं क्षयं च स्थानं च कर्शनोच्छेदनं तथा
सर्व्वोपायान् समादध्यादेतान्यश्चार्थशास्त्रवित् ॥

एवमन्योन्यसञ्चारं षाड्गुण्यं योऽनुपश्यति ।
स बुद्धिनिगलैर्बद्धैरिष्टं क्रीडति पार्थिवैः ॥[1]

True it is that the exponents of the theory of expediency in ancient India declared :

तावत् परो नीतिमान् स्याद्यावत् सुबलवान् स्वयम् ।
मित्रं तावच्च भवति पुष्टाग्नेः पवनो यथा ॥[2]

But does not this doctrine of political morality contain certain and universal truth ? In spite of the tangled mass of rules of International Law, is there any respectable state in Europe to-day which does not live in a perpetual armed peace ? And where is that rule of International Law which in the stern realm of fact concedes equality of status to a tiny little state like Montenegro, or a rather weak state like Servia, along with any of the "Big Five"? The retention of Egypt by England, the subordinate treaty of alliance entered into with Persia, Japan's persistent refusal to return Shantung to China are forceful illustrations of the statement of Sukracharyya.

As observed before, International Law in ancient India was based largely on religion and tacit consent but in numerous treaties and alliances entered into by various states, and in the developed conception of the Balance of Power we have also express sanctions of International Law. We have a definite idea of international consciousness in Kautilya's Arthasastra. In a passage the Vijigisu is advised to incite the "Circle of States" or मण्डल (a theory which probably owes its origin to the

---

[1] Arthasastra, VII. 18. Whoever is acquainted with the science of polity should clearly observe the conditions of progress, deterioration, stagnation, reduction and destruction, as well as the use of all kinds of strategic means. Whoever thus knows the inter-dependence of the six kinds of policy plays at his pleasure with kings, bound round, as it were, in chains skilfully devised by himself.

[2] Sukra, IV., vii, 89 : One should follow *Niti* or moral rules so long as one is powerful. People remain friends till then : Just as the wind is the friend of the burning fire.

love of symbolism of the ancient Indians), to preserve the balance of power against the overrapid growth of a *Madhyama King.*

मण्डलं वा प्रोत्साहयेत्—"अतिप्रवृद्धोऽयं मध्यमः सर्व्वेषां नो विनाशाय अभ्युत्थितः सम्भूयास्य यात्रां विहनाम" इति ।[1]

Although this international consciousness has for its basis interests of a sordid types till the force of public opinion is duly regarded by the Vijigisu or the conquering King in his dealings with the other states included within the circle of states. Thus, if he thinks that the circle of states would be enraged against a friendly state, for giving up its "sovereign" state, then the conquering King should keep quiet :

मध्यमश्चेत्स्वमित्रं मित्रभावि लिप्सेत, पुरुषान्तरेण सन्दध्यात्—"सापेक्षं वा नार्हसि मित्रमुच्छेत्तुम्" इति वारयेदुपेक्षेत वा—"मण्डलमस्य कुप्यतु स्वपक्षवधात्" इति ।[2]

If it is conceded that "laws" governed the relations between different states, the further question arises whether International Law in ancient India was a law regulating the relation between states or the conduct of Kings ? The answer to this question depends upon the general character of ancient Indian monarchy. It has been repeated many times that Grotius's Law of Nations was a law regulating the conduct of princes while the inestimable services of Vattel towards International Law consisted in his advocacy of the rules of International Law as guiding not princes but states in their mutual dealings, as also in his presentation of a developed body of rules relating to Neutrality. Hindu monarchy has been sanctified by the halo of divinity but the Hindu King could not at any time, like Charles I of England, declare that *Rex is Lex* and not *Lex is Rex*, nor could

---

[1] Arthasastra, VII., 18. [2] *Ibid.*

he proclaim like Louis XIV at the height of his power, "*L'état c'est moi.*" Though divine origin was attributed to him, the Indian monarch remained a mere servant of the Community, "the first servant of the state"; unlike the Roman "imperator," he was to all intents and purposes a trustee of the state. That was his position from the time of the Atharvaveda to the days of Kautilya when imperialism was at the noontide of its power and a ruthless policy of conquest and further conquest was urged upon the monarchs, by the Arthasastras. The King had to take a coronation oath in which he had to promise without mental reservation that he would see to the prosperity of the country, look upon it as Brahma and undertake to abide by all laws dictated by ethics or not opposed by politics.

प्रतिज्ञास्त्वामिवोऽसवो मनसाकर्म्मणा गिरा,
पालयिष्याम्यहं भौमं ब्रह्मइत्येव चासकृत् ।
यश्चात्रधर्म्मो नीत्योक्तो दण्डनीतिव्यपाश्रयः ।
तमशङ्कः करिष्यामि सर्व्वशो नकदाचन ॥[1]

The conception of the King as a salaried official of the state is an established truth according to Manusamhita, Sukracharyya and the Agnipurana.[2] Even an avowed imperialist like Kautilya recommended a virtuous king to address his army just on the eve of a battle thus :

"तुल्यवेतनोऽस्मि ; भवद्भिः सह भोग्यमिदं राज्यम् ;
मयाऽभिहितः परोऽभिहन्तव्यः"[3]

"I am a paid servant like yourselves; this country is to be enjoyed by me together with you; you have to strike the enemy specified by me." This

---

[1] Mahabharata : Santi-Raj, LXIX., 106-107.

[2] *Vide* Carmichael Lect., III (*b*), 1918.

[3] Arthasastra, X., 3.

theory about the trusteeship of the monarch receives further confirmation from the various theories about the origin of the state—even the "social contract theory" being clearly discernible in the Mahabharata, the Agnipurana and the Arthasastra of Kautilya. Thus, International Law in ancient India dealt not with the princes alone but with the subjects of all states as well. It is interesting to note here that in a voluminous dissertation, Grotius argued against the view that sovereignty, always and without exception, belonged to the people. Just as an individual may give himself up to slavery, he says, so may a people subject itself completely to one or more persons. In certain cases such submission will be advantageous. If it is objected that free men are not articles of commerce, Grotius replies that the liberty of an individual is one thing and the liberty of the nation of which he is a part another. According to Hindu ideas on the other hand, the personality and the sovereignty of the state stood for the personality and the sovereignty of the prince.

A general outline of International Law and Custom in ancient India has been attempted in the following pages. It will be shown that rules of International Law in various forms existed in ancient India. Admittedly, these rules were not perfect, nor did they cover rules relating to such important subjects as maritime warfare, blockade, law relating to contraband, as well as rules of private International Law relating to such important topics as extradition, and naturalisation; but the imperfections of International Law in ancient India should not blind one to the very fact of its existence. The translation of the Code of Manu into various European languages has led to the reluctant admission by some European writers that mitigations of horrors in warfare were advocated by the whole of the Aryan family of nations. To some authors like Philipson, the ideal of warfare set forth in Manu's Code was not actually followed in practice and he therefore condemned the ancient Indians to eternal perdition: their conception was high, their practice was low. In the following pages an attempt will be made to prove that practice generally conformed to the ideal excepting when the supreme need of the state overbore all moral considerations. If protection of state interest can condemn a nation to hell, then many nations of antiquity as well as of modern times will find a safe abode in that dismal and uninviting region.

CHAPTER I

Sources of International Law

Interstatal relations owe the English title "International Law" to Jeremy Bentham. Hugo Grotius called his book, "De jure belli ac pacis"; Puffendorff christened his work, "De jure natural et gentium"; Balthazar Ayala named his work, "De jure et officis Bellicis"; while Vattel wrote on "the Law of Nations or the Principles of Natural Law." Bentham in his "Introduction to the Principles of Morals and Legislation" (1789) made the following observation:

"The word 'International Law,' it must be acknowledged, is a new one, though it is hoped sufficiently analogous and intelligible. It is calculated to express in a more significant way that branch of law which goes by the name of the law of nations; an appellation so uncharacteristic that were it not for the force of custom, it would apply rather to internal jurisprudence. The Chancellor D'Aguesseau has already made, I find, a similar remark: he says that what is commonly called *droit des gens* ought rather to be termed *droit centre les gens*" (XVII, 25). The Hindus gave no special name to the science of interstatal relations or the modern science of International Law. They were firm believers in "*Desadharma*," they knew that a regulative science of international rules alone could accelerate interstatal intercourse and consequently internal prosperity; but the rules of international law according to their ideas had a better place in a science of polity, directing the activities of the sovereign of a sovereign state rather than in a separate treatise like the *Consolato del Mare* of the mediæval ages.

The four "eternal divisions of knowledge" according to the *Arthasastras*, "were *Anvikshikee, Trayee, Vartā* and *Dandaniti*,"[1] paving the way to happiness. Some of the great thinkers went so far as to assert that *Dandaniti* was the sole[2] source of knowledge and within this *Dandaniti* were included the rules and customs governing international intercourse and interstatal relations.

International Law in ancient as well as in modern times is based upon the sociability of the human nature directed by specific human needs and interests. The guiding motive of International Law, looked at from this point of view, is the utility or the satisfaction of collective needs and interests of states whether intellectual, moral or material. This theory of utility has been very forcefully brought out by the *Agnipurana*;[3] "No king becomes a friend or foe without sufficient cause, or without a due regard to his own interests for the sake of amity or discord." This then is the *basis* or foundation of International Law.

Writers frequently confuse the *sources* of International Law with its *basis* or *foundation* on the one hand and the *evidences* or witnesses to its existence on the other.[4]

The primary sources of International Law, according to modern jurists are (1) custom based on tacit consent

---

[1] & [2] Kamandaka, § ii, 5.

आन्वीक्षिकीं त्रयीं वार्त्तां दण्डनीतिश्च पार्थिव:। तद्विद्यैस्तत् क्रियोपेतैश्चिन्तयेद्विनयान्वित:।

आन्वीक्षिकी त्रयी वार्त्ता दण्डनीतिश्च शाश्वती। विद्याश्चतस्त्रएवैता योगक्षेमाय देहिनाम्

एकैव दण्डनीतिस्तु विद्येत्यौशनसी स्थिति:। तस्यान्तु सर्व्वविद्यानामारम्भा: समुदाहृता: ॥

[3] Agnipurana, CCXXXIII, 20.

Cf. also Story (Conflict of Laws, § 35) on p. 62 and Bentham's Works, VIII., 538.

[4] For example, Westlake (I., 14-15) makes "custom and reason," the two sources of International Law. He confuses one of its sources with a means of interpretation. And Oppenheim (I., n. 22) justly remarks that "reason is a means of interpreting law, but it cannot be called into existence."

and imitation;[1] (2) conventions or express agreements by means of treaties of an international character. The ancient Hindus understood the first source by *Desadhi-dharma* or *Dharma* in general, for example, Sukracharyya defines Desadharma as "custom which may or may not owe its origin to the Srutis but is always followed by the people in different climes"[2] . . . Various meanings have been attached to the expression *Dharma*. Dhammapada was so bewildered with their vastness and complexity that he exclaimed, "for those that are enveloped there is gloom, for those that do not see, there is darkness, and for the good it is manifest, for those that see there is light; even being near those that are ignorant of the way and the *Dharma* do not discern anything."[3] One thing at any rate is certain: that from the time of the Rigveda onward, *Dharma* meant both "Law" and "custom."[4]

The well-known definition of Dharma given in the Rajadharma-Prakaran of the Santiparva of the Mahabharata bears repetition: "No one in discoursing on righteousness can indicate it accurately. Righteousness was declared for the advancement and growth of all creatures. Therefore that which leads to advancement and growth is Righteousness. Righteousness was declared for restraining creatures from injuring one another. Therefore that is Righteousness which prevents injury to creatures. Righteousness is so called because it upholds all creatures. Therefore that is Righteousness

---

[1] Pollock: Sources of International Law, 2 Col. L. R. (1902), 511-24. Pomeroy, §§ 31-46.

कल्पित श्रुतिमूलो वामूलो लोकैर्धृतः सदा ।
देशादिधर्म्मः स ज्ञेयो देशे देशे कुले कुले ॥

[2] Sukra, IV., iii., 64.

[3] The S. B.E. X (ii), 144.

[4] McDonald and Keith: Vedic Index.

which is capable of upholding all creatures. Some say that Righteousness consists in what has been inculcated in the *Srutis*. Others do not agree to this. I do not censure them that say so. Everything again has not been laid down in the *Srutis*."[1]

No student of Indian antiquity has yet suggested this all-embracing definition of Dharma to be a subsequent interpolation and it very forcibly points out that Dharma or custom is indeed the basis of all righteousness whether in the dealings of a man towards his fellowmen or that of one sovereign state towards another sovereign state. Thus, the ancient Hindus recognized the truth of the well-known maxim of Pindar "that custom is the king of all things."[2]

The second primary source of International Law has been stated as conventions or express agreements by means of *treaties* of an international character. Unfortunately for us, like the treaty of an international character between Rameses II, King of Egypt ("the

---

[1] Mahabharata, Santi-Raj, CIX., 8-13, Pratap Ray's translation.

ताद्दशोऽयमनुप्रश्नो यत्र धर्म्मः सुदुर्विदः।
दुष्करं चापि संख्यातुं तर्केणात्र व्यवस्यति ॥
प्रभवार्थाय भुतानां धर्म्मप्रवचनं क्रतं ।
यः स्यात्प्रभवसंयुक्तः सधर्म्म इति निश्चयः ॥
"अहिंसा सत्यमक्रोधस्तपो दानं दमो मतिः ।
अनसूयाऽप्यसामर्थ्यामनीर्षा शीलमेवच ॥
एषधर्म्मः कुरुश्रेष्ठ कथितं परमेष्टिना ।
ब्रह्मणा देवदेवेन अयम् चैव सनातनः ॥
अस्मिन्धर्म्मे स्थितो राजन्नरो भद्रानिपश्यति ।
श्रौतो वधात्मको धर्म्मः अहिंसापरमार्थिकः ॥"
धारणाद्धर्म्ममित्याहुर्धर्म्मेण विधृताः प्रजाः ।
यः स्यादहिंसासंयुक्तः स धर्म्म इति निश्चयः ॥

[2] Attributed to Pindar by Herodotos, Bk. III., 38 (νομου παντων βασιλεα).

Pharaoh who knew not Joseph ")[1] and Khitasir, the King of the Hittites, we have no treaty of an international character in ancient India. We have various kinds of treaties defined and classified in the Arthasastras between the sovereign states of a *mandala*, we have instances of treaties or alliances and intercourse with foreigners, *e.g.*, Selukos Nikator, Antiochos Soter, Ptolemy Philadelphos, but they do not bequeath to us treaties with the stamp of International Law. Probably the ancient Hindus trusted too much to custom and probably they looked upon Dharma with the eyes of an ancient Hellene towards "the law of Nature." Thus Aristotle says:

"Customary laws have intrinsically more force, and pertain to more important matters than written laws; and that a man may well be a safer ruler than the written laws, but not safer than the customary law."[2] Thus when Creon accused Antigone of breaking the laws of the state, she replied that those laws were not ordained by Zeus, or by Justice who dwells with the Gods below:

> Cr. Now, tell me thou—not in many words, but briefly—knewest thou that an edict had forbidden this?
>
> An. I knew it; could I help it? It was politic.
>
> Cr. And thou didst indeed dare to transgress that law?
>
> An. Yes; for it was not Zeus that had published me that edict; not such are the laws set among men by the Justice who dwells with the Gods below; nor deemed I that thy decrees were of such force, that a mortal could override the unwritten and the unfailing

---

[1] Brügsch: Egypt under the Pharaohs, Vol. II, pp. 71-76.
Petrie: History of Egypt.
See Breasted: Records of Ancient Egyptian History.

[2] Politics, III., 16-9, ̓ετι κυριώτεροι καὶ περὶ κυριωτερῶν κατὰ γράμματα νόμων οἱ κατὰ τὰ ̀εθη ει'σιν, 'ὼστ' ει' των κατὰ γράμματα 'ὰνθρωπος 'ὰρχων. 'ασφαλέστερος,'αλλ'ου'-τῶυ κατὰ τὸ εθος.

> statutes of heaven. For their life is not to-day, or yesterday, but from all time; no man knows when they were first put forth."[1]

The evidences or witnesses of International Law in ancient India are many and various. These may broadly be classified into (*i*) the evidences of the Dharmasastras, (*ii*) the evidences of the Arthasastras, those of the (*iii*) Puranas and lastly (*iv*) of inscriptions. We have very little trace of interstatal relations during the Vedic times. We have only glimpses of a state in formation in the Vedic age—the Vedic monarch stood midway between a tribal chief and a territorial king, but the negative evidence of the Vedas stands us in good stead in proving the existence of International Law in ancient India. We get no examples of blood-curdling warfare, nor do we find the *Dasyus* or the *Dasas* absolutely outside the pale of law. Although the Aryan conquerors and colonizers called them "अकर्म्मन्" (a-karman), अब्राह्मण (a-brahmana) and अव्रत[2] (a-brata, *i.e.*, "lawless") still their struggle for existence was not embittered by the use of inhuman methods of warfare; the sacred pages of the Vedas are not disfigured by cannibalism and although we have absolute proof of the use of "poisoned arrows,"[3] still it is not proved that they were exclusively reserved for the aborigines.

Rules of International Law based on *accepted principles of morality* were promulgated in the Dharmasastras, *e.g.*, Manu Smriti, Yagnavalka, Apastamba, etc. Thus, in Chapter VII of the Code of Manu we have a glimpse

---

[1] Sophocles: Antigone, 450 *seq.* tr. Philipson.

[2] R. V., I., 51, 8; I., 175, 3.
R. V., VI., 14, iii.
R. V., IX., 41, ii.

[3] R. V., VI., 75, xv.
A. V., VI., 6, vii.
A. V., V., 18, viii.

of the Kautilyan theory of the "Mandala," or "the circle of states," an evidence of international intercourse in the appointment of diplomatic agents and we have also the accepted rules of humane method of warfare fully stated as well as rules relating to chivalry, enemy person and enemy property. We have humane laws of warfare as well as rudiments of what we now call "a Science of Politics" stated in the Santiparva of the Mahabharata, while warfare in the two Epics, the Ramayana and the Mahabharata, seems to have been conducted on the accepted principles of interstatal morality of a very high order.

Rules of International Law drawn from principles of expediency broadbased upon 'political considerations' find their suitable place in the Arthasastras. Almost the same rules relating to the "circles of states," intercourse between them, and rules relating to the sixfold policy, *viz.*, *sandhi* (peace), *vigraha* (war), *ásana* (observance of neutrality), *yâna* (marching),[1] *samsraya* (alliance) and *dvaidhibhava* (making peace with one and waging war with another) have been stated and re-stated in almost all their works. There were other writers of the Arthasastras (besides Kautilya, Kamandaka and Sukra) dealing with the same topics or allied topics but their works have been lost. We can gather scraps of information about them from the authors of various extant Arthasastras, such for instance, Kautilya, Kamandaka and Sukracharyya. Prof. Bhandarkar of the Calcutta Univer-

---

[1] There is a difference of opinion as to whether all these six expedients should govern the interstatal relations of the circle. Kautilya however votes for all the six.

सन्धिविग्रहासनयानसंश्रयद्वैधीभावाष्षाड्गुण्यम्। इत्याचार्य्याः

"द्वैगुण्यं" इति वातव्याधिः, सन्धिविग्रहाभ्यां हि षाड्गुण्यं सम्पद्यते" इति।

"षाड्गुण्यमेवैदवस्थाभेदात्" इति कौटिल्यः॥

sity has framed a list of the authors of the Arthasastras preceding Kautilya[1] :—

Schools.

1. Manavah.
2. Barhaspatya.
3. Ausanasha.
4. Parasarah.
5. Ambhiyah.

Individual Authors.

6. Bharadvaja.
7. Visalaksha.
8. Parasara.
9. Pishuna.
10. Kaunapadanta.
11. Vatavyadhi.
12. Bahudantiputra.
13. Katyayana.
14. Kaninka Bharadvaja.
15. Dirgha Charayana.
16. Ghotamukha.
17. Kinjalka.
18. Pishunaputra.

The most outstanding witness of International Law and Custom of ancient India is Kautilya, who has been identified by scholars with Chanakya, the Prime Minister of Chandragupta Mauryya. His Arthasastra is interesting from many points of view—not the least among them is its close analogy to rules of International Law laid down by mediæval jurists, for example, Grotius, Ayala and Rachel. As an evidence of International Law, Kautilya's Arthasastra has two obvious limitations: Firstly, he is a ruthless exponent of the principle of expediency, although it will be shown in subsequent chapters of

[1] Carmichael Lectures, pp. 89-90.

this thesis, that Kautilya's diplomacy is based on the universally followed doctrine of state-necessity. Secondly, the Arthasastra of Kautilya deals exclusively with warfare on land and does not therefore enable us to construct a body of rules relating to important topics such as blockade or contraband. It does not also deal with subjects of vital interest such as naturalisation and extradition. The Arthasastra of Kautilya was followed by Kamandaka and Sukracharyya, who along with Kautilya were the advocates of the utilitarian school of political philosophy. Many references relating to peace and war are to be found in their works as well as in the Agnipurana which from its own evidence is a book written at a time when the Tantricism was at its height.

Besides the rules directly relating to interstatal relations in the Arthasastra, we have in the Sukranitisara, evidence of private instructions given by individual states to their armed forces—rules of military discipline[1] some of which are not followed by the civilised nations of the world even to-day, *e.g.* :—

(1) The king should station troops near the village but outside it. And there should be no relationship of debtor and creditor between the village-folk and the soldiery.

---

[1] ग्रामाद्बहि: समीपेतु सैनिकान् धारयेत् सदा ।
ग्राम्यसैनिकयोर्न स्यादुत्तमर्णाधमर्णता ॥
चण्डत्वमाततायित्वं राजकार्य्ये विलम्बनम् ।
अनिष्टोपेक्षणं राज्ञ: स्वधर्म्म परिवर्ज्जनम् ॥
त्यजन्तु सैनिका नित्यं सल्लापमपि वा परै: ।
नृपाज्ञया विना ग्रामं न विशेयु: कदाचन ॥
स्वाधिकारिगणस्यापि ह्यपराधं दिशन्तु न: ।
मित्रभावेन वर्त्तध्वं स्वामिकृत्ये सदाखिलै: ॥
सूज्ज्वलानिच रक्षन्तु शस्त्रास्त्रा वसनानि च ।
अन्नं जलं प्रस्थमात्रं पात्रंवह्वन्नसाधकम् ॥
शासनादन्यथाचारान् विनेष्यामि यमालयम् ।

Sukra, IV., vii., 379, 381-83.

(2) The troops should always forsake violence, rivalry, procrastination over state affairs.

(3) They should never enter the village without a "royal permit."

(4) They should never point to the defects of their commander, but should always live on friendly terms with the whole staff.

(5) The troops will remain not only responsible for their personal arms and uniforms but also for their provisions and their cooking utensils.

(6) They were subjected to martial law if they intrigued with the enemy and were required to take an oath of allegiance which ran thus—" I shall kill the troops who will act otherwise."

CHAPTER II

International Status or Persons in International Law

"A state has been defined by Lawrence, as a political community, the members of which are bound together by the tie of common subjection to some central authority, whose command the bulk of them habitually obey......This central authority may be vested in an individual or a body of individuals ; and though it may be patriarchal it must be more than parental."[1]

If we analyse the above definition of the state we get the following characteristics of a sovereign state, the 'subject' of International Law :—

(1) It must have a government which receives the *de facto* allegiance from its subjects.

(2) It must be a sovereign independent state.

(3) It must exhibit reasonable promise of durability.

(4) It must possess definite territories.

(5) It must be recognized as a member of the family of nations.

In other words, a sovereign state that is a member of the modern European family of nations must possess *some degree of civilisation* and must occupy a *fixed territory.*

We have dim reference of a state so early as in the Vedic period. The *Samiti* which elected the Vedic

---

[1] Lawrence : Principles of International Law, p. 55.

king elected him the "King to the *Rasthra*," *e.g.*, in the election *gatha* from the Atharvaveda :[1]

> आ त्वाहार्षमन्तरभूर्ध्रुवस्तिष्ठाविचाचलत् ।
> विशस्त्वा सर्वा वाञ्छन्तु मा त्वद्राष्ट्रमधि भ्रशत् ॥
> ध्रुवोऽच्युतः प्र मृणीहि शत्रून्छत्रूयतोधरान् पादयस्व ।
> सर्व्वा दिशः संमनसः सध्रीचीर्ध्रुवाय ते समितिः कल्पतामिह ॥

"We welcome thee gladly. Be steady and do not falter. The whole *vis* want you. Do not tumble down from the state. Fixed and never falling, crush and trample down enemies or those who behave like enemies. Every quarter, *i.e.*, everybody assembled with one mind is honouring you : the Assembly here is appointing you for permanence." We have the traditional list of sixteen "**महाजनपदाः**" in the Pali works[2] such as :—

1.	Anga	9.	Kuru
2.	Magadha	10.	Panchala
3.	Kasi	11.	Machchha
4.	Kosala	12.	Surasena
5.	Uajji	13.	Assaka
6.	Matta	14.	Avante
7.	Cheti	15.	Gandhara
8.	Vanisa	16.	Kamboja

From the time of the Vedas and onward, the states of India grew in size and in importance till we come to the Mauryya period of Indian history, when Asoka had relations not only with four kingdoms of the South but also with principalities outside the borders of India,

[1] A.V., 6-9-2. I am indebted for this sloka to one of Mr. Jayaswal's soul-stirring articles in the Modern Review.

[2] Vinaya, II., 146.
Anguttara, I., 213 ; IV., 252, 256, 260.
Jataka, V., 316; VI., 271.
The Carmichael Lectures (1918), p. 48

and it does not require the ingenuity and the perseverence of an erudite scholar to prove that there were states, either country states or city states, in existence during the historic period in India.

1. *A state must have a government which receives the* de facto *allegiance from its subjects.*

Whether we accept the divine origin of the state as propounded by the *Aitareya Brahmana*,[1] the Mahabharata[2] or the Manusamhita[3] or we agree with the theory of Kautilya[4] that the state is a human creation, we see very clearly that the states in ancient India, whether republican or monarchical in character, had governments which received the *de facto* allegiance of the subjects. This has been beautifully expressed by Manu,[5] the apostle of the theory of the Divine origin of Kingship :

> " Punishment governs all created beings, punishment alone protects them, punishment watches over them when they sleep ; the wise declare punishment (to be identical) with law......................
> If the King did not, without tiring, inflict punishment on those worthy to be punished, the stronger would roast the weaker, like fish in a pit.
>
> The crow would eat the sacrificial cake and the dog would lick the sacrificial viands, and ownership would not remain with any one, the lower ones would (usurp the place of) the higher ones." (Bühler's translation)—Manu, VII., 19-20.

---

[1] Aitareya Brahmana, I., iii., 14. [2] Mahabharata, Raj-Santi, Sec. 59.

[3] Manu, VII., 3. [4] Arthasastra, I., 13 :—

तत्र येऽनुप्रशंसेयुः तानितरस्तं च प्रतिषेधयेत्—"मात्स्यन्यायाभिभूताः प्रजा मनुं वैवस्वतं राजानं चक्रिरे। धान्यषड्भागं पण्यदशभागं हिरण्यं चास्य भागधेयं प्रकल्पयामासुः। तेन भृता राजानः प्रजानां योगक्षेमवहाः तेषां किल्बिषमदण्डकरा हरन्ति। योगक्षेमवहाश्च प्रजानाम्। तस्मादुञ्छषड्भागमारण्यका अपि निवपन्ति—तस्येदं भागधेयं योऽस्मान्गोपायतीति।

[5] दण्डः शास्ति प्रजाः सर्व्वा दण्ड एवाभिरक्षति। दण्डः सुप्तेषु जागर्त्ति दण्डं धर्म्मं विदुर्बुधाः॥
समीक्ष्य स धृतः सम्यक् सर्व्वा रञ्जयति प्रजाः। असमीक्ष्य प्रणीतस्तु विनाशयति सर्व्वतः॥
यदि न प्रणयेद्राजा दण्डं दण्ड्येष्वतन्द्रितः। शूले मत्स्यानिवापक्ष्यन् दुर्व्वलान् बलवत्तराः॥
अद्यात्काकः पुरोडाशं श्वा वलिह्याद्धविस्तथा। स्वाम्यं च न स्यात्कस्मिंश्चित् प्रवर्त्तेताधरोत्तरम्॥

2. *It must be a sovereign independent state.*[1] Sovereign states are those which are fully autonomous and independent. The attributes of sovereignty according to Kautilya are—" the king, the minister, the country, the fort, the treasury, the army, and the friend."[2] From a passage in Kāmandaka,[3] we learn however, that Maya one of the authors of the Nitisastras, described four only of the states of the *Mandala*, or the " Circle of States " as ' sovereign states ' :

> " These four, namely, the *Vijigisu*, the *Ari*, the *Madhyama* and the *Udasina* have been said to be the principal components of a Mandala. This is the Mandala of four Sovereigns described by Maya conversant with Political Science."

The Mandala or the " Circle of States " has been described at some length by (*i*) Manu [4] and at great length by (*ii*) the authors of the Nitisastras for instance by Kautilya,[5] Sukracharyya[6] and Kāmandaka [7] as well as (*iii*) by the Agnipurana.[8] The number of foes and allies inside this मण्डल (mandala) varies. Generally speaking however, twelve Kings formed a Mandala, *viz.* :—

(*i*) *Vijigisu* or the Sovereign in the centre.

(*ii*) the five Kings whose dominions lay in front of the Vijigisu, *e.g.* :—

(*a*) *Ari*, the enemy,

(*b*) the friend of the Vijigisu (मित्रप्रकृतिः),

---

[1] The authorities are divided on the question whether sovereignty is an essential characteristic of the state. Among those who answer in the negative are Laband, Meyer, Oppenheim ; among those who answer in the affirmative are Borel, Bornhak, Merignhac.

[2] स्वाम्यमात्यजनपददुर्गकोशदण्डमित्राणि प्रकृतयः. A. S., V., ch. 6.

[3] Kamandaka : Nitisara, VIII., 20.

[4] Manu, VII, 155 et ffg.

[5] Kautilya, Bk. VI., Ch. 2, Shama Shastri, tr., pp. 322-24.

[6] Sukra.

[7] Kamandaka, Section VIII.

Agnipurana, CCXL.

(*c*) the enemy's friend (अरिमित्रं),

(*d*) the friend's friend of the Vijigisu (मित्रमित्रं),

(*e*) the friend's friend of the Enemy (अरिमित्रमित्रं).

(*iii*) In the rear of the Vijigisu there were—

(α) *Parshnigraha* or a rearward enemy,

(β) *Âkranda*, a rearward friend,

(γ) *Pârshnigrahasara*, an ally of the rearward enemy, and

(δ) *Âkranadasara*, an ally of the rearward friend.

(*iv*) Besides these we have (*a*) the *Madhyama* (the mediator) and (*b*) the *Udasina* (the neutral).

Thus it will be observed that the four states (*b*) the friend of the Vijigisu, (*d*) the friend's friend of the Vijigisu and the (β) *Âkranda* as well as the (δ) *Âkrandasara* were not wholly sovereign states. The Vijigisu controlled their activities and maintained the balance of power within the Circle of States.

नेमिमेकान्तरान्राज्ञः कृत्वा चानन्तरानरान् ।[1]
नाभिमात्मानमायच्छेत् नेता प्रकृतिमण्डले ॥

Each of these three states possesses the five elements of sovereignty, such as the minister, the country, the fort, the treasury, and the army and these are not therefore vassal states. It is noticeable however that they lack in the sixth attribute of sovereignty, *viz.*, "a friend" and Kautilya says "that it needs no commentary to understand that the three Circles of States having the enemy of (the conqueror) the Madhyama King, or the neutral King at the centre of each of the three circles are different from that of the conqueror."

अनेन मण्डलपृथक्त्वं व्याख्यातं अरिमध्यमौदासीनानाम् ।

Besides these protectorates or "spheres of interest," we have another kind of state known by the modern

---

[1] A. S., VI., 2.

phraseology of a "client state." The duties of the client state have thus been described by Kautilya :[1]

"He (the King of a client State) should behave himself like a servant to his master by serving the protector's *occasional* needs. Forts and other defensive works, 'acquisition' of kings, celebration of marriages, installation of the heir-apparent, commercial undertakings, capture of elephants, construction of covert places for battle, marching against an enemy, and holding sports—all these he should undertake only with the permission of the protector. He should also obtain the protector's permission before making any agreement with the people settled in his country or before punishing those who may run away from his country............He should not accept the offer of a good country even from a friend......He should also help the protector as much as he can. On all occasions of worshipping gods and of making prayers, he should cause his people to pray for the long life of his protector."[2] This is the true picture of such a client state as the kingdom of Kamrupa during the time of Harshavardhana, or perhaps a kingdom like modern Korea under the enlightened guidance of Japan.

3. *It must possess definite territories.*

Every king must be a territorial monarch, *i.e.*, he must not be a mere tribal chieftain. Of the seven elements of sovereignty, "the king, the minister, the country, the fort, the treasury, the army and the friend," *the country*

---

[1] Shama Sastri, pp. 323-324.

[2] Arthasastra, V., 2. 17.

Shama Sastri's translation, pp. 377-378.

लब्धसंश्रयः समयाचारितवद्भर्त्तरि वर्त्तेत । दुर्गादीनि च कर्माण्यावाहविवाहपुत्राभिषेकाश्वपण्यहस्तिग्रहणसत्त्रयात्राविहारगमनानि चानुज्ञातः कुर्वीत । स्वभूम्यवस्थितप्रकृतिसन्धिमुपघातमपसृतेषु वा सर्वमनुज्ञातः कुर्वीत । दुष्टपौरजानपदो वा न्यायवृत्तिरन्यां भूमिं याचेत······उचितां वा मित्राद्भूमिं दीयमानां न प्रतिगृह्णीयात् । ···········यथाशक्ति चोपकुर्यात् । दैवतस्वस्तिवाचनेषु तत्परा आशिषो वाचयेत् । A. S., VII., 15.

occupies a very prominent place. The minister, the fort, the treasury and the army have all a *pied à terre* in the country.

4. *The state in ancient Indian polity was not identified with the monarch.* A Hindu monarch could not like Louis XIV exclaim "*L'état c'est moi*" (I am the state). From very early times, the ancient Hindu monarch considered himself merely a custodian of the interests of the people. He was नरपति (protector of the people), भुपति (protector of the country). The Mahabharata regards the king as the highest servant of the community.

वलिष्ठेन शुल्केन दण्डेनाथापराधिनाम्

शास्त्रानीतेन लिप्सेथा वेतनेन धनागमम् ।

Mahabharata-Santi-parvam, LXXX., 10.

"A pure sixth part of the produce of the soil, 'fines and forfeitures' collected from offenders, taxes demanded in accordance with the Shastras (law) as your *wages* (**वेतनेन**) shall constitute your revenue." So we find also in *Sukraniti*, I., 188 :—

> "God has created the king though master in form, the servant of the people *getting his wages in taxes* and this for the protection and the growth (of the people) in all classes."

Says Kautilya

प्रजासुखे सुखं राज्ञः प्रजानां च हिते हितम् ।
नात्मप्रियं हितं राज्ञः प्रजानां तु प्रियं हितम् ॥

The trust character[1] of the Hindu monarch has also been very beautifully expressed by the Agni Purana :

> "The house of a monarch who lives for the amelioration of the condition of his subjects, is the heaven itself.........The king takes as his own share a sixth part of the income of his subjects good or bad

[1] The trust character of the Hindu monarch has been very forcibly pointed out by Mr. Jayaswal and Prof. Bhandarkar.

in exchange for his good government ; ....The king shall punish the wicked and the evil doers and in lieu of that, people shall justly pay him revenue.........The king should make good the loss to the owner, the price of an article stolen by a thief and on such an occasion the king shall reimburse himself out of the salaries of his police officers." [1]

5. *Lastly, the sovereign state must be a member of the family of nations.* This idea of a family of nations has held sway over the minds of men at all times. Thus, the Greeks, the most polished nation of antiquity looked upon all non-Hellenes as mere "barbarians," beyond and outside the pale of Greek religion. This exclusive frame of mind has been very well illustrated by Martin. In China there was a bond of sympathy between the various constituent states, but active hostility against the "barbarians." In the middle of the seventh century B.C. the Tartars of the north-west presented themselves in the court of Tsin, requesting a treaty of peace and amity and humbly offering to submit to be treated as vassals of the more enlightened Power. 'Amity,' exclaim-the prince, 'what do they know of amity ? The barbarous savages ! Give them war as the portion due to our natural enemies.' [2]

Even in our own day, races and nations outside the pale of the European family of nations are entitled to the protection of International Law merely by the application of the doctrine of *legibus soluti, legibus vivimus,* so that such an enlightened nation as the British do not feel the least compunction in using dumdum bullets against the African savages on the ground that they are not subjects of International Law. Herein lies the superiority of international usage of ancient India over the

---

[1] Ag. P., CCXXIII., 12. 14. 22.

[2] W. A. P. Martin : Traces of International Law in Ancient China.

international custom or usage of even the most enlightened nations of the modern world. The "अटवीदल" translated as 'wild tribes' by Mr. Shama Sastri were outside the 'circle of states' and yet not only were they not regarded as outlaws but Kautilya counselled even alliance with them, *e.g.* :—

सन्धिविग्रहक्रमहेतुभिर्वा चेष्टेत ।
दूष्यामित्राटविकानुभयोरुपग्रह्णीयात् ।
एवयोरन्यतरं गच्छन् स्तैरेवान्यतरस्य व्यसने प्रहरेत् ।
द्वाभ्यामुपहितोवा मण्डलापाश्रयस्तिष्टेत् ॥[1]

Kamandaka goes even further and says that peace might safely be made with an अनार्य्य :

"A king true to his promises, an Aryya, a virtuous prince, an *Anaryya*, one having many brothers, a very powerful sovereign, and one who has come off victorious in many wars, these seven are said to be the parties with whom peace should be concluded."

Then again,[2]

"Peace should be made with an Anaryya, for even he meeting an enemy eradicates him like the son of Renuka destroying the Khatriyas."[3]

Thus, in ancient Indian polity there were various grades of subjects of International Law according as they made free or fettered exercise of the rights of sovereignty, either in internal or in external matters.

---

[1] A. S., XII., 4.

[2] Kam., IX., 42. सत्यार्य्यधार्म्मिकानार्य्य भ्रातृसंघातवान् बली ।

[3] *Ibid*, IX., 45. अनेकविजयी चेति सन्धेयाः सप्त कीर्त्तिताः ॥

* * * *

सन्धिः कार्य्योऽप्यनार्य्येण सम्प्राप्योत्सादयेद्धि सः ।
रेणुकायाः सुतइव मूलेष्वपि न तिष्ठति ॥

CHAPTER III

INTERCOURSE OF STATES

Amongst the peoples of the most distant antiquity there were practices, more or less systematic, relating to the interchange of embassies. Yet, Sir F. E. Smith, the Attorney-General of England, writing the most recent English book on International Law warned his readers against "tracing in the immunity of envoys the germs of a nascent humanity; it was an immunity involved in the necessity of international intercourse."[1] It is this necessity of intercourse that however gave birth to diplomacy, and intertribal or interstatal law. As societies advanced in the successive stages of evolution, treaties began to be established for the control of such international relationships. Mr. G. C. Wheeler[2] in a very recently published book, has ably proved interchange of embassies accompanied by established formalities and ceremonies between the various states of China in remote antiquity. The Tel-el-amarna and the Boghazköyi tablets undoubtedly prove the existence of temporary embassies in the world round Egypt and Syria. In the Fiji Islands intercourse between group and group in peace or in war is conducted through the medium of heralds who are considered inviolable at all times. In Greece and Rome diplomatic relationships reached a very high state of development. In ancient Indian polity diplomacy was considered the sheet anchor of international or interstatal relationship. The importance of diplomatic relationship is fully recognised by Manu. "The army

[1] F. E. Smith: International Law, Sept., 1918, p. 1.

[2] G. C. Wheeler: Traces of International Law in the Ancient Orient. *Cf.* also Rde Maulde-la-claviere: La diplomatic au temps de Machiaval.

depends on the official (placed in charge of it), the due control (of the subjects) on the army, the treasury and the (government of) the realm on the king, peace and its opposite (war), on the ambassador."[1] Then again: "For the ambassador alone makes (kings) allies and separates allies; the ambassador transacts that business by which (kings) are disunited or not." [2]

To Kautilya, the *pontifex maximus* of the school of political expediency, diplomacy meant the only means of preserving the balance of power, as the surest weapon of success in material welfare.

एकं हन्यान्नवा हन्यादिषुः क्षिप्तो धनुष्मता ।
प्राज्ञेन तु मतिः क्षिप्ता हन्याद्गर्भगतानपि ॥ [3]

In ancient India, we have traces of diplomatic agents from very early times—from the time of the Rigveda. Thus we have a passage in the Rigveda [4] in which Agni discharged the functions of an ambassador.

"अग्निदूतं वृणीमहे होतारं विश्ववेधसं अस्य यज्ञस्य सुक्रतं ॥"

Sāyana in his commentary said—"अग्निः देवानां दूत आसीत्"। Diplomatic agents in ancient India were divided into दूत and चार. दूत, an open spy, corresponded to modern envoys, चार on the other hand was 'a secret spy' holding the honourable position of an "international spy" of our times. The Taitareya Samhita first drew this distinction [5] between दूत and प्रहित. Sayana explained दूत as परसैन्यवृत्तान्तकुशलः and प्रहित as स्वामिना प्रेषितः पुरुषः. In one word, the

---

[1] Manu, VII., 65 अमात्येदं.........................
नृपतौ कोशराष्ट्रे च दूते सन्धिविपर्ययौ ॥

[2] *Ibid*, VII., 66. दूत एव हि संधत्ते भिनत्येव च संहतान् ।
दूतस्तत् कुरुते कर्म भिद्यन्ते येन मानवाः ॥

[3] Arthasastra: X., 6.

[4] R. V., I., 12.1.

[5] Taitareya, IV., 7. 1.

former represented the sovereignty of the state and the latter was a mere international spy having no *locus standi* whatever in a foreign country.

The qualifications of an ambassador were very high. They were chosen from amongst the most distinguished and honoured citizens. Sometimes those who had already held high civil or military appointments were nominated for legations, as an additional mark of honour and in recognition of their able services. Thus says Kautilya:

उद्धृतमन्त्रो दूतप्रणिधिः ।[1]

Thus, in Greece the *Proxenoi*[2] who had experience and knowledge of foreign affairs in their domestic duties as protectors of foreigners, were frequently sent on important diplomatic errands. Thus, in democratic England, even now, the foreign office does not admit in practice the democratic principle of "a career open to talents."

All the writers on international or interstatal relations laid great stress on the loyalty, honesty, intelligence and proficiency in the art of the statecraft on the part of ambassadors. When we remember the recent occasions of refusal on the part of modern states to receive what we may politely call "indiscreet" or "undiplomatic," ambassadors we cannot but applaud the wisdom of the ancient Hindu writers on polity in their categorical insistence on qualifications of a very high order on the part of ambassadors.[3]

So says Bhisma in the Mahabharata:

"An envoy should possess these seven accomplishments, *viz.*, he should be highborn, of a good family, *eloquent*, clever, *sweet-speeched*,

---

[1] Arthasastra, I., 16.

[2] Livy: XXXVII., 55, 56.

[3] See Hall: International Law, 7th ed., p. 239.

N.B.—A well-known instance of dismissal occurred in 1888, when Lord Sackville, the English ambassador at New York was given his passports and required to leave the country within three days. Lord Sackville had been asked to advise an unknown

faithful in delivering messages with which he is charged, and endowed with good memory."[1]

Thus says Manu :

"An ambassador is commended to a king (who is) loyal, honest, skilful, possessing a good memory, who knows the (proper) place and time (for action) (who is) handsome, fearless, eloquent."[2]

The Agni Purana repeats the same thing :

"The ambassador sent to represent the king at a foreign court should be a man of a very sharp intellect, sweet-voiced, possessing eloquence of speech and well-versed in the arts of diplomacy........."

A man intelligent, ingenuous, well-versed in the arts of war and scriptural knowledge and accustomed to the work of espionage and possessing a good retentive memory and eloquence of speech should be appointed an ambassador.[3]

It is curious to note in this connection that "eloquence" and "sweetness of speech" were regarded as the greatest qualifications for an ambassador at a time when the art of writing despatches had not so well developed. Thus, the *legatus* or an envoy in Rome was generally called an *orator*. In French it appears that *orateur* had the meaning of "ambassador" until the close of the fifteenth century.[4]

---

correspondent of English extraction and sympathies how to vote in the Presidential election of that year. He replied suggesting in a general way that the then government was friendly to England whereas Mr. Cleveland's intentions were unascertainable. In September 1915, Dr. Dumba, the Austro-Hungarian ambassador in Washington, was recalled on the ground, first, that he had proposed plans to his Government for instigating strikes in American factories producing munitions of war, and secondly, that he had employed an American citizen to carry official despatches secretly to Austria through the lines of her enemies.

[1] Mahabharata, Santi-Raj, LXXXV., 28.

[2] Manu, VII., 64.

[3] Agni, CCXLI., 7.

[4] Livy : I, 15, "Veientes pacem oratores Romam mittunt."
Virgil : Aeneid, XI., 331.
"Centum oratores prima de gente Latinos"

Cf. also the Greek word 'ἔκδικος and αὐ'τοκράτορες.

Permanent embassies were not probably known to the world before the Peace of Westphalia, 1648, which brought about the close of the devastating Thirty Years' War in Europe, ushered in a brighter day for independent statehood and laid the foundation stone of "modern" International Law. The Greek embassies were not permanent institutions, nor could the Roman *fetials* be regarded as precursors of modern resident embassies endowed with the theory of "extra-territoriality." In Ancient India, the *Duta* was entrusted with certain specific mission,[1] the conclusion of which ended his career as an *open* international agent whereas 'wandering' spies or *secret* agents collected information from various states under various *rôles*. They, in no way, represented the might of the state but they merely formed a secret service "without letting the public know that they had been so employed," and the kings took particular care "to prevent their mutual recognisance."[2]

Comparative exclusiveness of states till quite recent times, looked upon foreigners generally with an eye of suspicion and diplomacy as a periphrasis for intrigue. Thus, Louis XI of France regarded an ambassador as a sort of chartered spy in the court of each of his powerful neighbours. "If they lie to you, lie still more to them"[3] was his general instruction to his ambassadors. Sir Henry Wotton's cynical definition of an ambassador was "a person sent to lie abroad for the benefit of his country." Coke in his famous *Institutes* praised King Henry VII "overmuch" because "he would not in his time suffer leiger ambassadors of any foreign king or prince within his realm, or he with them, but upon

---

[1] *E.g.*, the functions enumerated by Kautilya, I., 16.

[2] Agni Purana, CCXX., 17-24.

[3] Flassan : *Diplomatie Française*,, Vol. I, p. 247, cited by Lawrence, p. 246.

occasions used ambassadors."[1] So Grotius[2] affirms that a nation is not bound to receive resident embassies for such is unknown to ancient practice. The Agni Purana[3] gave vent to the same feeling of distrust in the following lines:

> "An ambassador is but an open spy and a spy is but an enemy travelling in the enemy's country, in the guise of a trader, a mendicant, or a strolling physician."

The institution of "foreign spies" claimed very great attention from ancient Hindu authors specially from Kautilya. His institution of spies has most likely never been rivalled in the world, excepting perhaps by the modern Germans.

"A kingdom has its roots in spies and secret agents," says Bhisma, in the Mahabharata.[4] The same sentiment is also expressed by the Agni Purana:[5]

> "The spies are the king's eyes and men should be employed in espionage and secret service, without letting the public know that they had been so employed and care should be taken to prevent their mutual recognisance. They should guide themselves as merchants, physicians, astrologers, religious mendicants, and watch the strength and the armaments of foreign kings. The king should not trust the statement of a single spy unless corroborated by informations received on the subject from different sources."

Espionage was a recognized international institution in ancient Indian polity and diplomatic duels between "secret service" agents were established facts in state-raft. Thus we find in Kautilya,—"spies set up by foreign kings shall also be found out by local spies; spies

---

[1] Coke: Fourth Institutes, ch. 26.

[2] Grotius: II., 18. 3.

[3] Agni, CCXLI., 12.

[4] Mahabharata, Santi-Raj, LXXXIII.

[5] Agni, CCXX., 17-24.

by spies of like profession."[1] Furthermore, Kautilya says :

एवं मण्डलमात्मार्थं विजिगीषुर्निवेशयेत् ।
पृष्ठतश्च पुरस्ताच्च मित्रप्रकृति सम्पदा ॥
सर्वेच मण्डले नित्यं दूतान् गूढांश्च वासयेत् ।
मित्रभूतस्सपत्नानां हत्वा हत्वा च संहतः ।[2]

P. 302, Mysore Ed.

Spies have been divided by Kautilya into nine classes : each spy playing a rôle different from that of his confrêre:—

1. *Kapatica-chhatra* ... A spy under the guise of a fraudulent disciple.
2. *Udasthita* ... A spy under the guise of a recluse.
3. *Grihapatika* ... One playing the part of a householder.
4. *Vaidehaka* ... One assuming the rôle of a merchant.
5. *Tapasa* ... Representing an ascetic practising penances.
6. *Satri* ... A student spy.
7. *Tikshana* ... A firebrand spy never stopping at any act of incendiarism.
8. *Rasada* ... A poisoner.
9. *Bhikshuki* ... A mendicant woman.[3]

All these spies were recruited from various classes of society, and persons of diverse conditions of life were drafted for this relentless machinery of the state. They were to adopt various disguises and received

---

[1] Arthasastra, Shama Sastri's edition, p. 25.

[2] Thus the conqueror should, through the aid of his friends, bring the Circle of States under his sway both in his rear and in front......he should send messengers and spies to reside in each of the states composing the circle.. A. S., VII., 13.

[3] कापटिकोदास्थित गृहपतिकवैदेहकतापसव्यञ्जनान् सत्रितीक्ष्णरसदभिक्षुकीश्च.—1-10, p. 18, Mysore Ed.

a thorough training in the " institute of espionage."[1] The "असम्बन्धिन:" or those who have no सम्बन्ध or relationship, *i.e.*, orphans and who were अवश्यभर्त्तव्य by the state received special training as apprentices (सत्रिण" संसर्गविद्या "),[2] in the institute of espionage. The spies were duly honoured by the state and they had to take an oath—

("राजानं मांच प्रमाणं कृत्वा यस्य यदकुशलं पश्यसि तत्तदानीमेव प्रत्यादिशति ") [3]

This oath did not absolve the state-officials from demanding corroboration of the statements of the spies. According to both Kautilya and the Agni Purana, the statement of a spy must be corroborated from three different sources and if the statements disagreed, then punishment was to be meted out to the spies.

त्रयाणामेकवाक्ये सम्प्रत्ययः। तेषामभीक्ष्णविनिपाते तूष्णीं दण्डः प्रतिषेधोवा ॥[4]

Of these nine classes of spies, the तीक्ष्ण, the रसद, and the परिव्राजिक were called संचारा: or "wandering spies." No distinction of caste or creed or sex was observed in the appointment of persons for espionage. Thus says Kautilya:

एतया मुण्डा वृषल्योव्याख्याता:[5]

That is, the same rules applied to women with shaven heads as well as to men of the Sudra caste. It is to be observed however that envoys or दूत were, generally speaking, recruited from the Brahmin caste. Learning and literary accomplishments were required of them and Kautilya[6] says that they were, in general, Brahmans.

---

[1] तं सत्रिण: संस्थास्वर्पयेयु:—*Ibid*, 1-12, p. 20, Mysore Ed.

[2] *Ibid*, p. 20, l. 3.

[3] *Vide supra.*

[4] Kautilya: 1. 12, p. 21, l. 11-12, Mysore Ed.

[5] *Ibid*, p. 20, l. 8.

[6] *Ibid*, 1-16, p. 30, Mysore Ed.

"तं ब्रुयात्—दूतमुखा वै राजानस्त्वं चान्ये च। तस्मादुद्धृतेष्वपि शस्त्रेषु यथोक्तं वक्तारस्तेषामन्तावसायिनोऽप्यवध्याः। किमङ्ग पुनर्ब्राह्मणः।

The wandering spies did not know each other and once out of the institute they were not permitted to enter the precincts of their *alma mater* again.[1]

नचान्योन्यं संस्थास्ते वा विदुः

The same thing is also repeated by the Agni Purana :

"The spies are the king's eyes and men should be employed in espionage and secret service, without letting the public know that they have been so employed and care should be taken to prevent their mutual recognisance."[2]

The institute of spies was not only a training school but a bureau of information and spies conveyed news to this great national espionage-institute.[3] Its organization was perfect, it had a regular hierarchy of officials who invented a regular code of signs and signalling for the purposes of receiving and transmitting messages :

"तं भिक्षुकाः संस्थास्वर्पयेयुः। संस्थानामन्तेवासिनः संज्ञालिपिभिश्चारसञ्चारं कुर्युः।"[4]

The great 'institute of spies' was an octopus in the state trying to bring under its grasp all kinds of activity in the state. Truly, it finds its counterpart in M. Fouche's school during the First Empire in France, and in the dreaded German espionage colleges of our days.

Long before the galaxy of diplomats, assembled round the "peace" table at Vienna in 1815[5] and long

---

[1] Kautilya : I. 12.

[2] Agni, CCXX., 17-18.

[3] Kautilya : p. 20, Mysore Ed.

[4] *Ibid*, p. 21, l. 4-5, Mysore Ed.

[5] At Vienna (*according to rank*).
(*a*) Ambassadors and *nuncios*.
(*b*) Envoys, Ministers plenipotentiary.
(*c*) *Charges d'affaires.*

before Vattel classified diplomatic agents,[1] Kautilya had divided diplomatic agents into four classes :—

(*i*)	उद्धृतमन्त्रो दूतप्रणिधिः ।	(*i*)	*Duta.*
(*ii*)	अमात्यसम्पदोपेतो निसृष्टार्थः ।	(*ii*)	*Nisrishtarthah.*
(*iii*)	पादगुणहीनः परिमितार्थः ।	(*iii*)	*Parimitarthah.*
(*iv*)	अर्धगुणहीनः शासनहरः ।	(*iv*)	*Sasanaharah.*

The *Duta* corresponded to αγγελος of Greece, the *legatus* of Rome and the ambassador of the modern times ; the *Nisrishtarthah* has been wrongly translated as *charge-d'affaires*, because a *charge-d'affaires* is an inferior kind of diplomatic agent accredited not to sovereigns but to the ministers of foreign affairs[2] and he occupied the lowest rung in the diplomatic ladder both at Aix-la-Chapelle and at Vienna. The *Nisrishtarthas*, on the contrary, are envoys possessing ministerial qualifications. They probably resemble the αυτοκαροpες of Aristophanes[3]—the plenipotentiaries-ambassadors charged with the conclusion of a treaty. The *Parimitartha* can be identified with the plenipotentiaries of a century ago. The *Sasanahara* is an inferior kind of envoy.

The right to send ambassadors both in Greece and in Rome was not regarded as an absolute right. It rested either on treaty stipulations[4] or on an express permission obtained from the state to which the ambassador was to be sent. Secondly, only sovereign states were allowed to represent themselves by diplomatic agents. Likewise, in

---

[1] Vattel's classification. *Droit-des-gens*, Bk. IV., § 73.

(*a*) Ambassadors.

(*b*) Envoys.

(*c*) Residents.

(*d*) Ministers.

[2] Hertslet : Map of Europe by Treaty, Vol. I., pp. 62, 63.

[3] *Pace* 359. *Aves* 1595.

[4] For example, the clause in the Thirty Years Truce : Thuc., IV., 118.

Κπρυκι δεκαι πρεσβεια και ακολουθοις δποοσοις αν δοκπ, περι καταλυσεως τουπολεμου και δικων ες Πελοπουνπσον και 'Αθπυοξε οπουδας ειναι ωυοι και απιονοι, και κατα γην και κατα θαλασσα.

ancient India, ambassadors represented the might of the state. Thus, we have in the Ramayana :

ब्रुवन्परार्थं परवान्नदूतो वधमर्हति ।[1]

Kautilya holds the same view :

तं ब्रुयात्—दूतमुखावै राजानस्त्वं चान्ये च ।[2]

"Messengers are the mouthpieces of kings." The word "चान्ये च" meaning "not only of thyself but of all" is probably a courteous way of putting things, because Kautilya observes further on, that an ambassador need not care for the mightiness of the enemy, thereby conclusively proving the equality of all states big or small, so far as interstatal intercourse by means of diplomatic agents was concerned.

वसेदविसृष्टः प्रपूजयानोत्सिक्तः, परेषु बलित्वं नमन्येत ।[3]

The ambassador received instructions from the monarch and armed with his credentials he sought permission to enter the state to which he had been accredited. Instructions of ambassadors were either verbal or written.[4] शासन is the word for instructions in Kautilya's Arthasastra.

शासने शासनमित्याचक्षते । शासन प्रधानाहि राजानः, तन्मूलत्वात्-सन्धिविग्रहयोः [5]

"Thus writs are of great importance to kings because treaties and ultimata leading to war, depend on writs." Then again, one class of envoys is called शासनहरः because it used to convey royal writs.[6]

---

[1] Ramayana : Sundar, LII., 19.

[2] Arthasastra, I., 16., p. 30, Mysore Ed.

[3] *Ibid.*

[4] *Cf.* the Roman custom, Dig, XLVIII, 6 :
"Item quod ad legatos oratores comites ve attienbit,
Si quis eorum pulasse et Sive injuriam fecisse arguetcur."
Arthasastra, p. 70, II., 9.

[6] *Ibid*, I., 16 ; also *cf.* सुप्रतिविहितयानवाहनपुरुषपरिवापः प्रतिष्ठेत 'शासनमेव' वाच्यः पवनाववात्येवंस्वेदं प्रतिवाक्यमेवमतिसन्धातव्यम्."—p. 30., XV., 6.

The reception of an envoy was not an inherent right and therefore envoys must have obtained permission of entry from the sovereign to whose territory he had to go.

पराधिष्ठानमनुज्ञातः प्रविशेत्। शासनंचयथोक्तं ब्रुयात्।[1]

He was to stay on till he was allowed to depart वसेनविसृष्टः. Only on failure of a mission or when fear of death hung overhead could the envoy return home without permission.

The envoy was to see the minister of foreign affairs as was the custom, at any rate during the time of Kautilya. "The ministers shall have to consider all that concerns the parties of both the king and his army" and the Arthasastra casts upon the sovereign 'surrounded by his council of ministers,' the duty of receiving ambassadors.

"मन्त्रिपरिषदा सामन्तदूतं।[2]

The reception of the ambassador in ancient India, therefore, was an act of state, shrouded by pomp and ceremony. In Athens, ambassadors were received and despatched by the assembly of the people; in Rome, they announced their arrival to the Senate through a prior notification to the prætor at the temple of Saturn; in Carthage, they were first 'presented to the people and afterwards brought before the assembly of the people.' Foreign envoys failing to get permission to enter the state, to which they were accredited as diplomatic agents, were treated unceremoniously. According to Kautilya, they fell under the iron rule of the Superintendent of Passports and on failing to produce passports were liable to the highest fine. In Rome, they were regarded as

---

[1] Arthasastra, p. 30, XI., 16.

[2] Instructions in Grace were designated συυβολα, in Rome "tesserva hospitales." Arthasastra, p. 45, I., 12, Mysore Ed.

mere spies and punishable as such. Thus, the Illyrians before their final incorporation with Rome failed to get recognition as they failed to report themselves to the Senate and were treated with scant courtesy. The functions of an ambassador have been thus defined by Manu :—[1]

"An ambassador alone makes allies and separates allies; the ambassador transacts that business by which (kings) are united or not." According to Manu, therefore, the functions of an ambassador are those of the traditional diplomat. Kautilya adds to these functions other duties necessitated by the promptings of civilisation and the dictates of interstatal relationship:

प्रेषणं सन्धिपालत्वं प्रतापो मित्रसंग्रहः ।
उपजापसुहृद्भेदो गूढ़दण्डातिसारणम् ॥
बन्धुरत्नापहरणं चारज्ञानं पराक्रमः ।
समाधिमोच्चो दूतस्य कर्मयोगस्य चाश्रयः ॥[2]

Thus, his functions were (1) transmission of messages, (2) maintenance of treaties, (3) issue of *ultimatums*, (4) breaking of peace—all the legitimate duties of a modern ambassador. Besides these, intrigue formed a second set of duties—intrigues worthy of the mediæval type of ambassadors like Count Gyllenbourg[3] in London or Prince of .Cellarmare[4] at Paris, *viz.*—(*a*) sowing dissension among friends, (*b*) fetching secret force, (*c*) carrying away by stealth relatives and gems, etc.

Even a modern ambassador under the hospitable roof of the "hotel" supported by the theory of "extra-territoriality"

---

[1] Manu, VII., 64.

[2] Arthasastra, I., 13.

[3] Count Gyllenbourg, the Swedish Minister in England abetted in 1717 a conspiracy to overthrow George I and to set up the Old Pretender on the throne of England.

[4] The Prince of Cellarmere, the Spanish Ambassador at Paris threw himself into the vortex of a conspiracy to seize the Duke of Orleans and proclaim the King of Spain, Regent of France.

plots in secret, like perhaps the German Ambassador at Washington in 1917 and therefore, an astute politician like Kautilya rightly created distrust in the minds of kings and asked them to be on their guard not merely passively but also actively.

स्वदूतैः कारयेदेतत् परदूतांश्च रक्षयेत् ।
प्रतिदूतापसर्पाभ्यां दृश्यादृश्यैश्च रक्षिभिः ॥

Immunities of Diplomatic Agents.

Everywhere in antiquity, the person of the ambassador was regarded inviolable. Thus, when David's[1] ambassadors were sent back by the people of Ammon with one side of their beards clean shaven, it was felt universally throughout Israel that the limits of international morality had been reached. The attitude of the Greeks and the Persians has been very well illustrated by Herodotus:[2] Just on the eve of the "Persian Wars," Emperor Darius sent heralds to Athens and Sparta "to demand earth and water from them"—probably as a token of nominal subjugation to his power. The Athenians and the Spartans naturally grew very angry. The former threw the Persian heralds into the bathrum and the latter into a well bidding them take earth and water from thence. A thrill of horror seems to have passed throughout Sparta for Herodotus tells us that two Spartan nobles offered their lives in exchange for the lives of the Persian envoys. The Asiatic Darius, however, would not agree and he did not want to imitate the example of the Lacedæmonians in perpetrating an offence against the common laws of mankind.

There seems to be an universal consensus of opinion in ancient India that the person of a Duta was inviolable

[1] Samuel, X., 4.
Herodotus, VII., 136.

and he must on no account be killed. He was the representative of the sovereign who sent him to a foreign court and therefore statecraft and custom both forbade his punishment or death.[1] The Mahabharata[2] is very emphatic in its denunciation of sovereigns who committed the gross offence of killing an envoy. "A king should never slay an envoy under any circumstances. That king who slays an envoy sinks into hell with all his ministers. That king observant of Kshattriya practices who slays an envoy who faithfully utters the message with which he is charged causes the manes of his deceased ancestors to be stained with the sin of killing a fœtus."

नतु हन्यात्नृपो जातु दूतं कस्यांश्चिदापदि ।
दूतस्य हन्ता निरयमाविशेत् सचिवैः सह ॥
यथोक्तवादिनं दूतं क्षत्रधर्मरतो नृपः ।
योहन्यात् पितरस्तस्य भ्रुणहत्यामवाप्नुयुः ॥

The *Nitivakyamrita* declared that a *duta* should never be killed even if he was a *Chandala*, while the *Nitiprakasa* gave vent to the prevailing sentiment by saying that even if an ambassador was guilty of a grievous wrong he could not be put to death.[3] Kautilya, however, is not so clear about the inviolability of diplomatic agents. Thus, according to him a displeased enemy to whose court an ambassador was accredited, might be told that messengers were the mouthpieces of kings and therefore *dutas* of Brahmin caste should not be killed:

"तं (to a displeased enemy), ब्रुयात्—दूतमुखा वै राजानस्त्वं चान्येच । तस्मादुद्धृतेष्वपि शस्त्रेषु यथोक्तं वक्तारस्तेषामन्तावसायिनोऽप्यवध्याः । किमङ्ग पुनर्ब्राह्मणः । परस्यैतद्वाक्यमेष दूतधर्म्म" इति ।[4]

---

[1] Ramayāna : Sundar Kandá, ब्रुवन् परार्थं परवान्नदूतोवध्यमर्हति, LII., 19; "राजधर्मविरुद्धश्च लोकवृत्तेश्च गर्हितम्," LII., 5-6.

[2] Santi-Rajdharma, LXXXV., 26-27.

[3] Nitiprakasa, III., 64.

[4] Arthasastra, I., 13.

As observed before, the juridical equality of states was recognized in ancient India and a *Duta* has been enjoined upon not to care for the mightiness of the enemy (परैश्ववलित्वं न मन्येत). A passage in the *Arthasastra* leads one to the belief that the *dutas* in ancient India were not liable to be killed but possibilities of punishments in cases of intimating an unfavourable order were not precluded. Thus says Kautilya :

ज्ञात्वा वसेदपसरेद्वा। प्रयोजनमिष्टमपेक्षेत वा। शासनमनिष्टमुक्त्वा बन्धवधभयादपि विसृष्टो व्यपच्छेदन्यथा नियम्येत ॥[1]

The testimony of the Ramayana confirms this statement of Kautilya, that under certain circumstances punishments could be awarded to envoys :

वैरूप्यमङ्गेषु कशाभिघातो मौण्ड्यं तथा लक्षण सन्निपातः।
एतान्हि प्रवदन्ति दण्डान्।

A *duta* in ancient India was therefore regarded inviolable so far as his life was concerned. He might under special circumstances be punished but such treatment was not sanctioned by Dharma just as in our day, national excitement has sometimes offered unmerited insults to ambassadors, *e.g.*, on the outbreak of the last great world war, the British embassy at Berlin was subjected to special maltreatment at the hands of the infuriated mob at Berlin.

We have little knowledge of the *civil* immunities of the *dutas* : probably the fact of their *non-residence* at the courts of foreign kings did not concede any *civil* immunities to them such as are enjoyed by ambassadors and other diplomatic agents of the present times. A passage in Kautilya affords very special immunities to "foreigners importing merchandise." They were

---

[1] A. S., I., 1. *Cf.* also the Ramayana, Sundar, LII., 15.

exempted from being sued for debts unless they were intimately connected with local associations.

परभूमिजं पण्यमनुग्रहेणावाहयेत्। नाविकसार्थवाहेभ्यश्च परिहारमायतिक्षमं दद्यात्। अनभियोगश्चार्थेष्वागन्तूनामन्यत्र सभ्योपकारिभ्यः।[1]

Such favours were no doubt shown for the advancement of the internal prosperity of a state but commercial intercourse with foreigners must have been regarded as one of the means of maintaining interstatal relationship and probably immunity from civil liability was conceded to diplomatic agents who represented the might of their respective states.

[1] Arthasastra, II., 16.

CHAPTER IV

THE ESSENTIAL RIGHTS AND DUTIES OF STATES

Sovereign states possess certain rights and duties. These are based largely on custom and therefore in ancient Indian polity, based on Dharma; others owe their origin to the independent character of a subject of International Law. Modern jurists have divided these Rights into:

1. The right of self-preservation.
2. The right of independence.
3. The right to exclusive jurisdiction over men and things within the territory of the state.
4. The right to commerce: and
5. The right of legal equality.

All these rights were possessed by the "*prakritis*"[1] of ancient India.

The right of self-preservation includes the right of preserving the integrity and inviolability of its territory with the corresponding duty[2] to commit what would ordinarily be regarded as an infraction of the Law of Nations. The Hindus held धर्म्मार्थकाममोक्षाणां प्राणाः संस्थिति-हेतवः and what was true of the individual was also true of the state.

Hence the desperate efforts for the preservation of the balance of power and the adoption of various policies which owe their origin to self-interest.

"When a king ever so vigilant and assiduous is assaulted by a sovereign stronger than himself, there is no escape for him as there is none for a deer under the claws

---

[1] For the doctrine of 'expediency' and 'Justice' *vide ante.*

[2] "Prakritis" were the sovereign-states.

of a lion."[1] It is then that the necessity for self-preservation "becomes instant, overwhelming, leaving no choice of means and no moment for deliberation."[2] Then the king may have recourse to *Kutajuddha* (कुटयुद्ध).[3] It is then that the "enemy has to be killed in wars whether conducted according to the rules of morality or against them," because, "one should follow *niti*, or moral rules so long as one is powerful. People remain friends till then; just as the wind is the friend of the burning fire."[4] The weak ruler of a soverign state for his very existence and the very life of the state should either (1) conclude peace or (2) take recourse to मन्त्रयुद्ध or (3) कुटयुद्ध. Thus says Kautilya,[5]

"तेषामन्यतममुत्तिष्ठमानं सन्धिना मन्त्रयुद्धेन कूटयुद्धेन वा प्रतिव्यूहेत। ....दुर्गं राष्ट्रं स्कन्धावारं वाऽस्य गुढ़ाशस्त्ररसाग्निभिः साधयेयुः सर्वतः पार्ष्णिमस्य ग्राहयेत्। अटवीभिर्वा राज्यं घातयेत्। तत्कुलीनावरुद्धाभ्यां वा हारयेत्।"

"When any one of these (conquerors) is on the point of rising against a weak king, the latter should avert the invasion by making a treaty of peace, or by taking recourse to the battle of intrigue, or by a treacherous fight in the battle field.........spies under concealment may capture the enemy's fort, country or camp with the aid of weapons, "poison" or "fire." They may harass the enemy's rear on all sides; and they may devastate the enemy's country through the help of wild tribes."[6]

The second right of a state is *the right of independence*. It flows as a necessary corollary from the

---

[1] Kam., X., 47.

[2] Webster in the "Caroline" Case (U.S.A. 1837); see Snows' *Cases*, 177, 178, and Westlake; I., 300.

[3] Sukra, IV., 725.

[4] *Ibid*, IV., 706.

[5] *Ibid*, IV., 376-77.

[6] Arthasaastra: Shama Sastri's translation, p. 462.

sovereignty of the state. The political condition of India, the absence of institutions such as the Papacy or the Holy Roman Empire, helped ancient India to realise this right of autonomy to a far larger extent than could have been perhaps possible in such a remote age. Thus, a state in India could maintain any form of government it liked, be it the predominant monarchical type or perhaps an oligarchy or even a republican form of government.[1]

The second characteristic of an independent state is that it exercises *exclusive jurisdiction* over all persons and property *within* its territorial limits and sometimes its jurisdiction is extended by the application of the doctrine of "*extra-territoriality*" over pirates and over its vessels on the high seas. A careful study of Kautilya's Arthasastra leaves the undoubted impression on the mind that the jurisdiction exercised by members of the "family of nations" in ancient India was ample and all-absorbing. Thus (*a*) they maintained absolute control over aliens within their jurisdiction. Amongst the primary duties of the sovereign, "the securing of affection of the foreigners both at home and abroad" finds the foremost place.

जतस्वपक्षपरपक्षोपग्रहः कार्य्यारम्भान् चिन्तयेत् ।[2]

(*b*) Emigration and immigration, two of the surest evidences of inter-statal intercourse, were recognized in ancient India. Thus we find that one of the duties of the "revenue collectors" was to investigate the causes of emigration and immigration through the agency of spies

---

[1] See the researches of Mr. Jayaswal (in Mod. Review, 1913). Read also the Carmichael Lectures: Lect. IV. "The Sangha Form of Government."

[2] Does परपक्ष mean foreign faction composed of the native population in a state? *Cf.* for instance, Whibley: The Parties and the Party System in Ancient Greece.

under the guise of householders. Then again, further on we read in Kautilya's Arthasastra :

"विगृहीतस्यान्यतो वा शक्यामि जनपदमपवाहयितुम् ।"[1]

(*c*) The state also never failed to exercise its jurisdiction when foreigners intrigued within its territory—they were either exposed or betrayed or killed with weapons, poison or by other means.[2]

Thus, the sovereign states not only controlled emigration and immigration, not only did they punish offenders guilty of treason against the might of the state but they also exercised jurisdiction over merchant vessels. The "superintendent of ships" (the नावध्यक्ष) demanded payment of tolls from all ships touching at harbours on their way :

"संयातीर्नाव: क्षेत्रानुगता: शुल्कं याचेत ।"[3]

(*d*) A foreigner had to protect himself with passports and on failure to do so, he had to pay the highest fine.[4]

समुद्रो जनपदं प्रवेष्टुं निष्क्रामितुं वा लभेत् ।
द्वादशपणममुद्रो जनपदो दद्यात् ।
कूटमुद्रायां पूर्व्व:साहसदण्ड: ।
तिरोजनपदस्योत्तम: ।[4]

(*e*) Travellers had also to provide themselves with passports or they were sure to be arrested and their property ran the risk of confiscation.

"दीर्घपथिकममुद्रं चोपग्राहयेत् ।"[5]
प्रत्यन्तेषु तरा: शुल्कमातिवाहिकं वर्त्तनीं च गृह्णीयु: ।
निर्गच्छतश्चामुद्रस्य भाण्डं हरेयु: ॥[6]

---

[1] Arthasastra, VIII., 1.
[2] *Ibid*, IX., 5.
[3] *Ibid*, II., 28.
[4] Arthasastra, II., 33.
[5] *Ibid*, II., 28.
[6] *Ibid*, II., 29.

(*f*) Pirates were of course liable to punishment. Pirate ships which were bound even for the country of an enemy, as well as those ships which had violated customs and rules of the port towns were destroyed.[1]

हिंस्रिका निर्घातयेत् । अमित्रविषयातिगाः पण्यपत्तनचारित्रोपघातिकाश्च ॥

It is very probable that pirate ships were destroyed by the ships of a maritime state and the very first duty of the superintendent of ships was to examine the accounts not only of ships on the high seas and on river-mouths but also upon lakes, natural or artificial.

The right of conducting commercial intercourse with foreign states was very frankly recognised : foreigners of reputation were allowed to land on seaports ; weather beaten ships were afforded generous hospitality and foreign merchandise was specially protected.

कृतप्रवेशाः पारविषयिकाः सार्थप्रमाणा च विशेयुः[2] मूढ़वाताहतां तां पितेवानुगृह्णीयात् ॥[3] परभूमिजं पण्यमनुग्रहेणावाहयेत् । नाविकसार्थवाहेभ्यश्च परिहारमायतिक्षमं दद्यात् ।[4]

This probably related to those natives who imported foreign goods into the country. But a curious passage of Kautilya throws a flood of light on the civil obligations of foreign debtors : Foreigners importing merchandise were exempted from being sued for debts.[5]

अनभियोगश्चार्थेष्वागन्तूनामन्यत्र सभ्यकारिभ्यः ।[6]

---

[1] *Ibid*, II., 28.

[2] Arthasastra, II., 28.

[3] *Ibid*.

[4] *Ibid*, II., 16.

[5] *Ibid*.

[6] *Cf*. the Agni Purana : CCXX., 17. "Without any regard to their honesty or wickedness the king should hospitably receive the foreigners arrived in his court, with a view to live under his protection. Such newcomers happening to be wicked men should not be trusted at all : but the king should buy their submission with annuities. Detectives shonld be employed to ascertain the character of all newcomers and foreigners in the state whom the king shall fill with honours in the event of their being deserving recipients."

This record of state-activity approximated modern usage but these rules of international custom might probably have been observed in the great Magadhan Empire of which Kautilya was the prime minister, but it might be contended on the other hand, that the Arthasastra gives expression to the customs and usages of the maritime states generally although probably, the officers on whom the observance of those customs and usages was cast by Kautilya were officers solely of the great Maurya Emperors.

Thus, the elementary rights of a state conceded by the sanctity of international usage are discernible in the sovereign states of India. Infractions, however, of these elementary rights were not uncommon. Such infractions known as "intervention" according to the phraseology of modern International Law took the form अभिवर्त्तनम् or war. Intervention has been defined by Oppenheim as "dictatorial interference in the affairs of a nation," the essence of which consists in the presence of force or threat of force and in the absence of consent. Interventions in ancient India were by no means unknown and we have instances of (*a*) interventions for preserving the balance of power by the circle of states, against a mighty *madhyama*.

"मण्डलं वा प्रोत्साहयेत्—अतिप्रवृद्धोयं मध्यम सर्व्वेषां नो विनाशाय अभ्युत्थितः सम्भूयास्य यात्रां विहनाम।" इति। तच्चेन्मण्डलमनुगृह्णीयान्मध्यमावग्रहेणात्मानमुपबृंहयेत्।[1]

"Or he may incite the Circle of States against the Madhyama by telling them: "This Madhyama king has grown very powerful and is aiming at our destruction: let us therefore combine and put an end to his march. If the circle of states is favourable to his cause then he may aggrandise himself by putting down the Madhyama."

[1] Kam., X., 5.

(*b*) Interventions to ward off an imminent danger accrued from the right of self-preservation above referred to, and were frequently resorted to.

(*c*) Interventions on grounds of humanity[1] have been justified by Sukracharyya.[2]

"Those kings who are devoid of morality and power should be punished, like thieves by the king who is powerful and virtuous."

The same view is held by Kamandaka:[3]

"The want of compassion on creatures, disaffection of the prakriti-mandala...............these and many others have been said to be the (prolific) sources of war."

Interventions at the request of the disaffected people have been justified both by Sukracharyya and by Kautilya.

Thus says Sukracharyya:[4]

"The king should surround and coerce the ruler whose army and friends have been lessened,..................*who is very much addicted to sense pleasures*, who is the plunderer of people's goods, and whose ministers and troops have been affected."

Kautilya as a great advocate of expediency advised a Vijigisu to march against an enemy whose subjects were being oppressed rather than against an enemy whose subjects were impoverished and greedy. The loyalty of the citizen towards the state has been fully recognised, and though like Aristotle, Kautilya was a great believer in hunger being the most potent factor of a revolution, he pressed his views even against the views of his teachers:

क्षीणलुब्धप्रकृतिमपचरितप्रकृतिं वेति ?—क्षीणलुब्धप्रकृतिं यायात्।
"क्षीणलुब्धा हि प्रकृतयः सुखेनोपजापं पीडां वोपगच्छन्ति। नापचरिताः

[1] Arthasastra, VII., 18.

[2] Sukra, IV., 845-46. (Sarkar.)

[3] *Cf.* the intervention of European powers, 1860, in the massacre of the Armenians.

[4] Sukra, IV., 498-500. (Sarkar.)

प्रधाना अवग्रहसाध्या" इत्याचार्य्याः। "न" इति कौटिल्यः—क्षीणलुब्धा हि प्रकृतयो भर्त्तरि स्निग्धा भर्त्तृहिते तिष्ठन्ति। उपजापं वा विसंवादयन्ति, अनुरागे सार्वगुण्यमिति। तस्मादपचरितप्रकृतिमेव यायात्॥

He observes further:

> क्षीणाः प्रकृतयो लोभं लुब्धा यान्ति विरागताम्।
> विरक्ता यान्त्यमित्रं वा भर्त्तारं घ्नन्ति वा स्वयम्॥[1]

[1] Arthasastra, VII., 5.

CHAPTER V

THE THEORY OF THE BALANCE OF POWER

The theory of the "Balance of Power" is based on the equilibrium of forces. It has been responsible for the maintenance of standing armies, for wearisome negotiations and for incessant wars. In most states of antiquity the principle of the balance of power was understood and often applied in practice. Hume in his Essays[1] traced the history of the theory of the balance of power to the Orient. "It is a question," said he, "whether the *idea* of the balance of power be owing entirely to modern policy, or whether the *phrase* only has been invented in later ages." Hume had before him the historic example of Greece only as perhaps representing the "magic east" and he came to the conclusion that to whatever causes we attribute the shifting of sides in all the Grecian republics, to jealous emulation or cautious politics, the effects were alike, and every prevailing power was sure to meet with a confederacy against it, and that often composed of its former friends and allies. The Peloponnesian league on the eve of the great Peloponnesian War complained not so much against the specific faults of commission or omission of the Athenian Empire as of her rapid growth of power and her concealed desire to undermine the autonomous independence of the Greek[2] City States. The story of the foundation and the decline of the ephemeral Spartan empire in Greece after the peace of Antalcidas only confirmed the proposition laid down by Hume. Demosthenes's oration for the Megalapolitans shows a refined sense of the theory of the

[1] Hume: Of the Balance of Power (Essays, Vol. I, 348-49).

[2] Thucydides: I., 23.

balance of power. Shortly after the peace of Callias, envoys from Megalapolis as well as Sparta reached Athens, each of them urging the Athenians to enter into an alliance with it. The Spartans reminded the Athenians of their old alliance between them against their common foe of Thebes. Demosthenes, however, took the side of the Megalapolitans and laid great stress on the fact that neither Sparta nor Thebes should be allowed to jeopardize the balance of power. "No man," said he, "will deny that it is for the advantage of Athens that both the Lacedæmonians and our Theban neighbours should be weak. But if we may form a conjecture from representations repeatedly made in our assembly, it appears that things are thus circumstanced—the Thebans will be weakened by the re-establishment of Orchomenus, Thespiæ and Platæa: the Lacedæmonians will become powerful again, if we subdue Arcadia and take Megalapolis. We must therefore mind that we suffer not the one people to grow mighty and formidable, before the other has become weak; that the power of Lacedæmon does not increase unobserved by us, in a greater degree than it is well for that of Thebes to be reduced. For we shall hardly say that we would have the Lacedæmonians as our rivals rather than the Thebans. Our solicitude is not concerned with this merely; for we are anxious that neither of them may have the means of injuring us; and so shall we enjoy the best security."[1] Demosthenes's oration failed to convince his countrymen. The result was Chæronea, the empire of Macedon and the end of the *politeia* in *Hellas*. The City State succumbed to the Country State.

In the history of Rome we do not find a clear enunciation of this doctrine of political equilibrium. Rome's advance was sure, her military successes were brilliant,

[1] Demos: Pro Megalapolis, IV-V., tr. Philipson.

her general policy and diplomatic conduct were subtle and all the states of the then civilised world fell a prey to the Roman policy of "divide et impera." The theory of the balance of power however had a feeble illustration in Hiero II, King of Syracuse, and extorted the warm admiration of Polybius.

Wars of the balance of power have devastated the fair countries of Europe many a time; the triple alliance fought Louis XIV successfully. The policy of Ferdinand followed by Richelieu and Mazarin was to remain Catholic at home and Protestant abroad so as to prevent the formation of a coalition against France. Louis XIV in his lust of ambition departed from that traditional French policy and the result was Utrecht and the years of tortuous European diplomacy. Napoleon I and Napoleon III and, lastly, the Kaiser Wilhelm threatened the supposed "finely equiposed" balance of power in Europe and the result is what all the world knows.

The theory of the balance of power held a very prominent place in ancient Indian statecraft. Thus the preservation of the balance of power by an ideal king was strongly advised by Manu.

"On the whole, eight-fold business and the five classes (of spies) on the good will or enmity and the conduct of the circle (of neighbours he must) carefully recollect."[1]

Further on Manu observes:

"By all the (four) expedients a politic king must arrange (matters so) that neither friends, nor neutrals, nor foes are superior to himself."[2]

"Separation," says Sukracharyya, "is the best of all methods or policies of work."[3]

---

[1] Manu, VII., 154.
[2] *Ibid*, VII., 177.
[3] Sukra, IV., 592.

Just as Sovereignty is possible only with assistance—as a single wheel can never move,"[1]— so the ideal king was to place himself at the centre to hold the balance of states in his hands.

नेमिमेकान्तराद्राज्ञः कृत्वा चानन्तरानरान् ।
नाभिमात्मानमायच्छेत् नेता प्रकृतिमण्डले ॥[2]

"Throwing the circumference of the circle of states beyond his friend's territory and making the kings of those states as the spokes of that circle, the conqueror shall make himself the nave of that circle."

Now what is a *mandala* or the "circle of states"? It consists of twelve kings, according to Kautilya.[3] (1) The *Vijigisu* is the fountain of policy. The king whose territory adjoins the territory of the Vijigisu is the (2) *Ari*. Separated by the Ari from the territory of the Vijigisu is situated the territory of (3) मित्रप्रकृति the friend of the Vijigisu. Close to his territory is the state of the (4) enemy's friend (अरिमित्रम्). Next to him stands the (5) Vijigisu's friend's friend (मित्रमित्रं) and next to him the (6) *Vijigisu's* enemy's friend's friend (अरिमित्रमित्रं). Likewise in the rear of the enemy there happen to be situated the territories of (7) a rearward enemy (पार्ष्णिग्राहः), next (8) a rearward friend (आक्रन्दः), then an ally of the rearward enemy *parshnigrahasara* (पार्ष्णिग्राहसारः), (9) and an ally of the rearward friend (आक्रन्दसारः). (10)[4] [5]

"राजा आत्मद्रव्यप्रकृतिसम्पन्नो नयस्याधिष्ठानं विजिगीषुः । तस्य समन्ततो मण्डलीभूता भूम्यनन्तरा अरिप्रकृतिः । तथैव भूम्येकान्तरा मित्र-

---

[1] "सहायसाध्यं राजत्वं चक्रमेकं न वर्त्तते" Arthasastra, I., 6.

[2] Arthasastra, VI., 2.

[3] According to Maya the *Vijigisu*, the *Ari*, the *Madhyama* and the *Udasina* are the four principal components of a *Mandala*.

[4] According to Puloma and Indra, the *Vijigisu*, the *Arimitram*, the *Parshnigraha*, the *Madhyama* and the *Udasina* constitute what is known as a *Mandala* of six monarchs.

[5] The *Udasina*, the *Madhyama* and the *Mandala* of the *Vijigisu* taken together

प्रकृतिः। अरिसम्पद्युक्तः सामन्तः शत्रुः। * * * * तस्मान्मित्र-मरिमित्रं मित्रामित्रं अरिमित्रं चानन्तर्येण भूमीनां प्रसज्यते पुरस्तात्। पश्चात् पार्ष्णिग्राह आक्रन्दः पार्ष्णिग्राहासार आक्रन्दासार इति।"[1]

Besides these eight kings who were the "protectorates" of either the *Vijigisu* or the *Ari* there remained two other kings within the circle, who might be regarded as neutrals,—the territory of the one lying close to the territories of both the *Vijigisu* and the *Ari* was the state of the *Madhyama* king, while the twelvth member of the circle had his territories situated beyond the territories of all the other kings within the circle (the *Udasina*).

अरिविजिगीष्वोर्भूम्यनन्तरः संहतासंहतयोरनुग्रहसमर्थो निग्रहे च। संहतयोर्मध्यमः। अरिविजिगीषुमध्यानां बहिः प्रकृतिभ्यो बलवत्तरः संहतासंहतानामरिविजिगीषुमध्यमानामनुग्रहे समर्थो निग्रहे चासंहतानामुदासीनः॥[2]

It is difficult to understand the distinction between a **मध्यमः** and a **उदासीनः**! It is certain, however, that the **उदासीन** whose dominions lay beyond the territories of either the **विजिगीषु** or the **अरि** and who was very powerful, capable of helping both and of withstanding each of them individually was identical with what we now call a "neutral" power. The dominions of the Madhyama king, on the other hand, lay contiguous to the states of both the **विजिगीषु** and the **अरि**. He was also a very powerful king like the **उदासीन** but unlike him his interests had greater chances of clashing

constitute the *Mandala* of the Twelve Kings mentioned by Usanas.

[1] Arthasastra, VI., 2.

अरिर्मित्रमरेर्मित्रं मित्रमित्रमतःपरम्।
तथारिमित्रमित्रञ्च विजिगीषोः पुरःस्थिताः॥
पार्ष्णिग्राहः स्मृतः पश्चादाक्रन्दस्तदनन्तरं।
आसारावनयोश्चैव विजिगीषोस्तु मण्डलम्॥

Kam., VIII., 16-17.

[2] *Ibid*, VI., 2.

with the interests of the विजिगीषु and therefore the "theory of enmity by distance" receives firm proof when we read in the Arthasastra that accession of power to the Madhyama must always be regarded with suspicion by the विजिगीषु not simply as a possible future enemy inciting the circle of states but also as a source of impending peril.

"मध्यमश्चेद्विजिगीषोः मित्रं मित्रभावि लिप्सेत मित्रस्यात्मनश्च मित्राण्युत्थाप्य मध्यमाच्च मित्राणि भेदयित्वा मित्रं त्रापयेत। मण्डलं वा प्रोत्साहयेत्—"अतिप्रवृद्धोऽयं मध्यम सर्व्वेषां नो विनाशाय अभ्युत्थितः सम्भूयास्य यात्रां विहनाम।"[1]

It is very probable that the *Madhyama* is a king who is just neutral but anxious to interfere or mediate. So he must not be allowed to grow very strong. If he curries favours with the third and the fifth states of the *Mandala*, states friendly to the *Vijigisu*—then the *Vijigisu* must be friendly with the *Madhyama*, but if the latter seeks amity with the second, the fourth and the sixth, that is, the enemy states—then the *Vijigisu* must make friends with his allies and try to win the उदासीन or the neutral king.[1]

A *Vijigisu* may also remain in peace by firmly preserving of the balance of power within the "circle of states." Thus says Kautilya:

"परतः प्रवृत्तकर्मारम्भो वा ताभ्यांसंहितः कर्मसु वृद्धिः प्राप्स्यामि; शत्रुप्रतिबद्धं वा शत्रुणा सन्धिं कृत्वा मण्डलं भेत्स्यामि।"

Then again, the policy of separation underlying the doctrine of the balance of power has been recommended to a king whose possessions lie intermediary to those of two powerful kings. He may first seek protection either of the more powerful or perhaps of the more reliable, king and then he may begin to set one of them against the other.[2]

---

[1] Arthasastra, VII., 18.

[2] Bk. VIII., 2.

The theory of the balance of power received the impetus of expediency and like the same doctrine translated into actual usage by Emperor Napoleon III, it became a cloak for further ambitious designs and for further conquests. Hence, by the adoption of the doctrine and by its steady application in practice, the kings in ancient India "endeavoured to pass from the state of deterioration to that of stagnation and thence to progress."[1]

[1] Arthasastra, Bk. VII., 1.

CHAPTER VI

TREATIES AND ALLIANCES

Peace formed one of the six attributes of statecraft.[1] It has been defined by Kautilya[2] as an agreement with pledges "पणबन्धः सन्धिः." "Those actions by which the powerful foe becomes friendly constitute treaty," is Sukracharyya's definition.[3]

"A *Sandhi*," says the Agni Purana,[4] "consists in a compact entered into by two foreign kings regarding a point at issue whereas war means the settlement of a difference at the point of the sword." Peace according to the Hindus was the normal state of interstatal relationship. A great exponent of the principle of expediency like Kautilya says that the acquisition and security of property depend upon peace and industry. "शमव्यायामौ योगक्षेमयोर्योनिः"[5]

A classification of treaties is not generally attempted by writers of modern International Law as "such instruments range over the whole variety of international relations"[6] Martens however divided treaties into *political* and *social*. This division though not exhaustive is very suggestive and will be found to correspond to the two great divisions into which the treaties in the Arthasastras

---

[1] सन्धिं च विग्रहं यानमासनं च समाश्रयम् ।
द्वैधीभावं च संविद्यान्मन्त्रस्यैतांस्तु षड्गुणान् ॥

Sukra, IV., vii.. 234.

षाड्गुण्यस्य प्रकृतिमण्डलं योनिः
सन्धिविग्रहासनयानसंश्रयद्वैधीभावा षाड्गुण्यं इत्याचार्याः
षाड्गुण्यमेवैतदवस्थाभेदात् इति कौटिल्यः ।

[2] A. S., VII., 1.

[3] Sukra, IV., vii., 235.

[4] Agni, CCXXXIV., 17-11.

[5] A. S., VI., 2.

[6] Hall: International Law, 7th Ed., 371 n.

have been divided.[1] According to Kamandaka there are sixteen kinds of peace.

कपाल उपहारश्च सन्तानः सङ्गतस्तथा ।
उपन्यासः प्रतीकारः संयोगः पुरुषान्तरः ॥
अदृष्टनर आदिष्ट आत्मामिष उपग्रहः ।
परिक्रियस्तथोच्छिन्नस्तथा च परिभूषणः ॥
स्कन्धोपनेयः सन्धिश्च षोडशः परिकीर्त्तितः ।
इति षोड़शकं प्राहुः सन्धिं सन्धि विचक्षणाः ॥

(1) *Kapala Sandhi* has been defined by Kamandaka as peace between two parties having equal resources. कपालसन्धिर्विज्ञेयः केवलं समसन्धितः ।[2] Kautilya, however, takes an almost opposite view. According to him, *Kapala Sandhi* is the opposite of स्वर्णसन्धिः or golden peace (the सङ्गत सन्धिः of Kamandaka). So Kapala, in his opinion, is concluded on the condition of paying immense sums of money.[3]

सुवर्णसन्धिर्विश्वासादेकीभावगतो भवेत् ।
विपरीतः कपालःस्यादत्यादानाभिभाषितः ॥[4]

(2) उपहार is peace concluded by the offer of gifts. According to both Sukracharyya and Kamandaka this is the only form of peace. Thus says Sukra :[5]

एक एवोपहारस्तु सन्धिरेष मतो हितः ।
उपहारस्य भेदास्तु सर्व्वेऽन्ये मैत्रवर्जिताः ।

---

[1] F. D. Martens : I., §13. Fodéré (II., 920 ff.) divides treaties, considered as to their object, into *general* and *special*. This division seems somewhat arbitrary but it affords a convenient means of summary. Perhaps the most scientific classification of treaties is that which divides them into "executed," "transitory," or "dispositive" treaties on the one hand; and executory, continuing, or permanent treaties on the other. "An executory contract is one in which a party binds himself to do or not to do, a particular thing. A contract executed is one in which the object of the contract is performed and this says Blackstone, differs in nothing from a grant:" *per* Marshall, C.J., in *Fletcher* vs. *Peck*, 6 Cranch 136.

[2] Kam., IX., 2-4.

[3] *Ibid*, IX., 5.

[4] A. S., VII., 3.

[5] Sukra, IV., vii., 240-241.

अभियोक्ता बलीयस्त्वादलब्ध्वा न निवर्त्तते ।
उपहारादृते तस्मात् सन्धिरन्यो न विद्यते ॥

"There is thus only one kind of peace desired by the people and that is, 'gifts' and without gifts there is no other form of peace." The same sentiment is also expressed by Kamandaka.[1]

एक एवोपहारस्तु सन्धिरेतन्मतं हि नः ।

(3) *Santana Sandhi* is one which is based upon matrimonial relationship, established by the vanquished by giving his daughter in marriage to his adversary.

(4) *Sangata Sandhi* or golden peace is concluded by the settlement of amicable terms by the parties.

(5) *Upanyasa Sandhi* is so called because it brings matters to a conclusion according to a previously formed resolution. स उपन्यासकुशलैरुपन्यास उदाहृतः.

(6) प्रतीकार सन्धि is concluded by mutual good understanding and expectation, *e.g.*, the alliance between Sugrīva and Rāma.

(7) *Samyoga Sandhi* means a form of union entered into by two parties enjoying each other's confidence, for the performance of a common object.

(8) *Purushantara* is peace with hostages.

(9) *Adristapurusha Sandhi* is peace which requires the performance of some act without corresponding advantage.[2]

---

[1] Kam., IX., 21.

[2] Kamandaka, IX., 9.

त्वयैकेन मदीयार्थः सम्प्रसाध्यस्त्वसाविति ।
यत्र शत्रुः पणं कुर्यात् सोऽदृष्टपुरुषः स्मृतः ।

Kam., IX., 14.

Kautilya however explains "अदृष्टपुरुष सन्धिः" as "peace with no specified person to serve." The two writers differ considerably on this kind of peace.

(10) *Adista Sandhi* is peace by cession of territory.

(11) *Atmamisha Sandhi* is one in which a king with the flower of his army has to attend the conqueror when summoned. It is a kind of 'vassalage.'

(12) *Upagraha Sandhi* is one which is concluded by the surrender of everything else excepting the person of the vanquished.[1]

(13) *Pratikriya Sandhi* is peace with price, *i.e.*, when all the elements of sovereignty are set free by the offer of money.

(14) *Uchchinna Sandhi* is destructive peace concluded by large cession of territories.

(15) *Skandhopaneya Sandhi* is peace with indemnity by instalments.

(16) *Paribhusana Sandhi* is "usufructuary" peace—peace obtained by giving up the products of the whole territory.[2]

Kautilya in his *Arthasastra* divides treaties and agreements for peace into various kinds: (*i*) *Atmamisha*, (*ii*) *Purushantara Sandhi*, (*iii*) *Adrishtapurusha Sandhi*, (*iv*) *Parikraya*, (*v*) *Upagraha*, (*vi*) *Swarna Sandhi*, (*vii*) *Kapala*, (*viii*) *Adistha*, (*ix*) *Uchchinna Sandhi*, (*x*) *Paribhushana*, (*xi*) *Avakraya*. (*i*)—(*ix*) are included in the list furnished by Kamandaka. *Avakraya* means treaty by which the kingdom is set free by the payment of a part of the produce of the kingdom.[3]

---

[1] Kautilya however explains *Upagraha Sandhi* by peace with subsidy. "When peace is concluded by offering money capable of being taken on a man's shoulder it is called Upagraha. "स्कन्धोपनेयो वहुधा ज्ञेय:सन्धिरुपग्रह:."—A. S. VII., 3. But Kamandaka: "क्रियते प्राणरक्षार्थं सर्व्वदानादुपग्रह:."—Kam., IX., 16.

[2] Kamandaka, IX., 18: "सर्व्वभूम्युत्थितफलदानेन परिभूषण:." Kautilya considers परिभूषण a kind of peace concluded by the promise of paying more than the land yields: "फलातिभुक्तो भुमिभ्य: सन्धि: स परिभूषण: "—A. S., VII., 3.

[3] The definitions of the various kinds of treaties mentioned by Kautilya are quoted *in extenso* here below. It is to be observed, however, that the whole thing

Of these various forms of peace **आत्मामिष, पुरुषान्तर** and **अदृष्ट** require supply of troops by the vanquished to the conqueror. In the two forms of **आत्मामिष** and **पुरुषान्तर** a woman of high rank has been enjoined upon to be given as hostage. This condition is very humiliating as we gather from our knowledge of nations of antiquity in general. Thus we have it stated on the authority of Tacitus's *Germania* that to the Germans the idea of a woman being led into captivity was intolerable; and hence when the daughters of illustrious families were

---

is in rhyme. Is it probably because Kautilya found these forms of treaties sanctified by usage ?

स्वयं संख्यातदण्डेन दण्डस्य विभवेन वा।
उपस्थातव्यमित्येष सन्धिरात्मामिषो मत: ॥
सेनापतिकुमाराभ्यां उपस्थातव्यमित्ययम्
पुरुषान्तरसन्धि:स्यान्नात्मनेत्यात्मरक्षण: ।
एकेनान्यत्र यातव्यं स्वयं दण्डेन वेत्ययं।
अदृष्टपुरुष: सन्धिर्दण्डमुख्यात्मरक्षण: ॥
मुख्यस्त्रीबन्धनं कुर्य्यात् पूर्व्वयो: पश्चिमे त्वरिम्।
साधयेत्गूढ़मित्येते दण्डोपनतसन्धय: ॥
कोशदानेन शेषाणां प्रकृतीनां विमोचणम्।
परिक्रयो भवेत् सन्धि: एव च यथासुखम् ॥
स्कन्धोपनेयो बहुधा ज्ञेय: सन्धिरुपग्रह: ।
निरुद्धोर्देशकालाभ्यां अत्यय: स्यादुपग्रह: ॥

* * *

सुवर्णसन्धिर्विश्वासादेकीभावगतो भवेत्
विपरीत: कपाल: स्यादत्यादानाभिभाषित: ।

* * *

भूम्येकदेशत्यागेन देशप्रकृतिरक्षणं।
आदिष्टसन्धिस्तत्रेष्टो गूढ़स्तेनोपघातिन: ॥
भूमीनामात्तसाराणां मूलवर्जं प्रणामनम्।
उच्छिन्नसन्धिस्तत्रैष परव्यसनकाङ्क्षित: ॥
फलदानेन भूमीनां मोचणं स्यादपक्रय: ।
फलातिभुक्तो भूमिभ्य: सन्धि: स परिभूषण: ॥

A. S., VII., 3.

delivered as hostages, the most effective obligation was thereby engendered.[1] In earlier Roman History women—Roman matrons—were given as hostages. We read in Livy that when the Etruscan Lars Porsena withdrew his troops from Janiculum, and peace was concluded a number of Roman hostages, including maidens, had to be given. According to Livy's story, the camp of the Etruscans having been pitched near the Tiber, a young Roman lady named Cloelia, one of these hostages, deceiving the guards, swam over the river, amidst the darts of her enemy, at the head of a number of virgins, and brought them back all safe to their relations.[2]

Upagraha, *Suvarnasandhi*, and *Kapala* were three forms of peace concluded on the payment of money; while *Avakraya*, *Uchchinna Sandhi* and *Paribhusana* were three kinds of peace based on cession of territories.

Besides the eleven kinds of treaties mentioned above, there were also other kinds of agreements either with or without any binding forms or specific ends. Peace with no specific end is called अकृतचिकीर्षा and peace with binding terms is called कृतश्लेषणम्. Peace with no specific end besides self-preservation, is a renewed agreement of peace either with equal, inferior or superior powers according as rights of the parties are determined with respect to their respective positions. अपूर्व्वस्य सन्धेः सानुबन्धैः सामादिभिः पर्य्येषणं समहीनज्यायसां च यथाबलमवस्थापनमकृतचिकीर्षा ।[3]

When by the employment of friends (at the courts of each other) an agreement of peace is maintained and the terms are strictly observed so that there might not arise any difference of opinion, the peace is called कृतश्लेषणम् or peace with binding terms. "कृतस्य प्रियहिताभ्यामुभयतः

[1] Tacitus's *Germania*, 8.

[2] Livy, II. 13. *Cf.* also Virg.: Aeneid, VIII., 6. 51.

Arthasastra, VII., 6.

परिपालनं यथासम्भाषितस्य च निबन्धनस्यावर्त्तनं रक्षणं च 'कथं परस्मान्न भिद्येत इति' क्तश्लेषणम्" ॥[1]

Treaties have further been divided into (*i*) **समसन्धिः**, (*ii*) **विषमसन्धिः** and (*iii*) **अतिसन्धिः** according as the adoption of a "double policy" (**द्वैधीभाव:**) entails upon kings of superior, equal or inferior power, the payment of a greater, equal or less amount of profit in proportion to the army supplied.[2]

"द्वैधीभूतो वा कोशेन दण्डं दण्डेन कोशं सामन्तानामन्यतमाल्लिप्सेत्। तेषां ज्यायसोऽधिकेनांशेन समात्समेन हीनाद्धीनेनेति समसन्धिः। विपर्यये विषमसन्धिः। तयोर्विशेषलाभादतिसन्धिः।"[3]

The above kinds of treaties mark the cessation of hostilities. Besides them, we have instances of treaties of agreement entered into by kings in times of profound peace, such as treaties[4] for the acquisition of land or for colonization. The one is called **भूमिसन्धिः**, the other is called **अनवसितसन्धिः**; "त्वंचाहं च भूमिं लभावहे" इति भूमिसन्धिः.[5] Acquisition of territory might be made either from a wandering enemy (**चलमित्रात्**) or from a stupid king[6] (**बालिशात्**). The one would be an original mode of acquisition from wild tribes, because, the land in which they effected temporary settlements was in the eye of law mere *res nullius*; the second kind of treaty gave land to the 'conqueror' by that derivative mode of acquisition named, 'cession.' Acquisition of property by colonisation[7] would come under the head of acquisition of *res nullius* by

---

[1] Arthasastra, VII., 6.

[2] In this is to be seen the germ of that policy known as the subsidiary policy of Lord Wellesley.

[3] A. S., V., 7.

[4] Arthasastra, VII., 10.

[5] *Ibid*, VII., 10.

[6] *Ibid*, VII., 10: "बालिशात्प्राज्ञाद्वा भूमिलाभ इति? बालिशाद्भूमिलाभःश्रेयान्"

[7] *Ibid* VII., 11: "त्वं चाहं चशून्यं निवेशयावह इत्यनवसितसन्धिः"

occupation. The doctrine of effective occupation[1] seems to have been fully understood by Kautilya because he prefers a small piece of land not far to an extensive piece of land very far.

अल्पा प्रत्यसन्नामहती व्यवहिता वा भूमिरिति ?

अल्पा प्रत्यासन्ना श्रेयसी सुखा हि प्राप्तुं पालयितुमभिसारयितुं च भवति ; विपरीता व्यवहिता ।

Lands might also be acquired either by (*a*) compulsory sale or (*b*) voluntary sale. The treaty of peace by which a powerful king compels another to sell a portion of his land is called अनिभृतसन्धि:—"गुणवतीमादेयां वा भूमिं बलवता क्रयेण याचित:सन्धिमवस्थाप्य दद्यादित्यनिभृतसन्धि: ।[2] A king making a voluntary sale of land was to do so after mature deliberation and calm consideration.

"समेनवा याचित: कारणमवेक्ष्य दद्यात्—प्रत्यादेया मे भूमिर्वश्या वाऽनया प्रतिबद्ध: परो मे वश्योभविष्यति भूमिविक्रयाद्वा मित्र-हिरण्यलाभ: कार्य्यसार्थकरो मे भविष्यति इति" ।[3]

The sanctity of treaties and alliances was very fully recognized and Kamandaka advises a wise king not to

---

[1] The doctrine of effective occupation is of comparatively recent origin. It was introduced into International Law during the Sixteenth and the Seventeenth Centuries. It was a protest against the right of occupation by mere right of discovery by Spain and Portugal. The oft-quoted reply of Queen Elizabeth of England to Mendoza, the Ambassador of Philip II of Spain that she did not "acknowledge the Spaniards to have any title by donation of the Bishop of Rome" may be capped by the mocking questions of Francis I of France to Charles V of Spain: "By what right do you and the King of Portugal undertake to monopolize the Earth? Has father Adam made you his sole heirs, and if so, where is a copy of the will?" (Lawrence).

[2] Arthasastra, VII., 11. "When a king of equal power demands land from another as above, then the latter may sell it after considering 'whether the land can be recovered by me, or can be kept under control; whether my enemy can be brought under my power in consequence of his taking possession of the land; and whether I can acquire by the sale of the land friends and wealth enough to help me in my undertaking."

[3] *Ibid.*

enter into agreements of peace with twenty sorts of persons, *viz.*, (*i*) a young prince, (*ii*) a king in the process of senile decay, (*iii*) a king suffering from disease for a very long time, (*iv*) a king discarded by his relatives, (*v*) a cowardly sovereign, (*vi*) a sovereign surrounded by a circle of cowardly followers, (*vii*) a king full of greed, (*viii*) a king whose officers are greedy and covetous, (*ix*) a king who is under the influence of adverse fate, (*x*) one who has an exaggerated faith in chance, (*xi*) one who is famine-stricken, (*xii*) a king whose army is in mutiny, (*xiii*) a king who is in an unfamiliar land, (*xiv*) a king who has numerous enemies, (*xv*) a king who does not value opportunities, (*xvi*) a king who is devoid of truth and justice, (*xvii*) a king whose *prakritis* are in a state of revolt, (*xviii*) a king who is a great debauch, (*xix*) a king who has no stability of character or fixed resolve and (*xx*) a king who desecrates the gods and the Brahmans.[1]

Ample guarantees were demanded for the due fulfilment of the terms of the treaties and the observance of treaties depended on—

(1) **सत्यशपथः** (oath).
(2) **प्रतिभुः** (securities).
(3) **प्रतिग्रहः** (hostages).

---

[1] बालो वृद्धो दीर्घरोगस्तथा ज्ञातिबहिष्कृतः।
भीरुको भीरुकजनो लुब्धो लुब्धजनस्तथा॥
विरक्तप्रकृतिश्चैव विषयेष्वतिसक्तिमान्।
अनेकचित्तमन्त्रस्तु देवब्राह्मणनिन्दकः॥
दैवोपहतकश्चैव दैवचिन्तक एव च।
दुर्भिक्षव्यसनोपेतो बलव्यसनसङ्कुलः॥
अदेशस्थो बहुरिपुर्युक्तः कालेन यश्च न।
सत्यधर्मव्यपेतश्च विंशतिः पुरुषा अमी॥

Kam., IX., 13-16.

"सत्यं शपथो वा चलसन्धिः। प्रतिभुः प्रतिग्रहो वा स्थावरः" इत्याचार्याः। नेति कौटिल्यः— सत्यं शपथो वा परत्रेह च स्थावरःसन्धिः ; इहार्थ एव प्रतिभूः प्रतिग्रहो वा बलापेक्षः।"

A. S., VII., 17.

"My teacher," says Kautilya, "is of opinion that peace dependent upon honesty or oath is mutable, while peace with a security or hostage is immutable." Kautilya however differed from him and regarded oath as the basis of all treaties. It is for this world only that a security or hostage is required for strengthening the agreement. The value of oath governing the relations of man and man has been richly illustrated by the great epics; the admission of the ethical superiority of the oath not only in this but in the great hereafter by Kautilya, the great diplomat and astute politician as well as the high priest of the gospel of expediency proves conclusively that oath in a certain sense is the underlying basis of the whole body of the ancient law of nations. Honest kings of old according to Kautilya, concluded an agreement of peace merely by saying "संहितास्मः."[1] Treaties in Greece as also in Rome were conceived to be under the protection of the gods. Thus, Zeus in the recitals of the Iliad is represented as a witness to the sanctity of treaties. "Zeus, most glorious, most mighty and ye other immortal Gods! Whosoever shall first commit wrong contrary to their pledges, may their brains and their children's be dispersed on the ground, like this wine and may their wives prove faithless."[2]

Ceremonials were indispensable incidentals to a conclusion of peace and in ancient India according to Kautilya, kings made their agreement by swearing by fire, water, the plough, the brick of a fort or wall, the shoulder of an elephant, the hips of a horse, the front of a chariot, a weapon, seeds, scents, wrought gold or bullion gold and by declaring that these things would destroy and desert him who violates the oath.

---

[1] A. S., VII., 17.

[2] Iliad, III., 298-301.

"तस्यातिक्रमे शपथेन अग्न्युदकसीताप्राकार लोष्टहस्तिस्कन्धाश्वपृष्ठरथोपस्थशस्त्ररत्नबीजगन्धरससुवर्णहिरण्यान्यालेभिरे। हन्युरेतानि त्यजयुश्चैनं यः शपथमतिक्रामेत्" इति ॥[1]

An early account of the conclusion of a treaty is also given in the *Iliad*. It was the case of an agreement entered into by the Trojans and the Argives with regard to the combat for Helen between Menelaus and Alexander. First of all, the herald made an announcement in the city of the duel and of the preliminaries that were to ensue, and brought two lambs, some wine in a goat-skin bottle, a bowl and golden cups. "When all were assembled, the lordly heralds brought together the faith-ensuring pledges of the gods and mingled the wine in a bowl, and poured water over the hands of the princes. Then Atreides cut off the hair from the heads of the lambs, which was distributed by the heralds amongst the chiefs of the Trojans and the Achaeans. Atreides raising his hands then offered up this prayer: 'Father Zeus that rulest from Ida, most glorious, most mighty, and thou Sun that beholdest all things, and hearest all things and ye Rivers and thou Earth, and ye that in the underworld punish men deceased, whosoever has taken a false oath; be ye witnesses, and watch over the faith-ensuring pledges.'"

Ζευ πατερ, Ιδηθεν μεδεων, κυδιστε, μεγιστε,
Ηελλιος θ,'ος παντ Εφορας και παντ' επακουεις,
Και Ποταμοι και Γαια, και οι υπενερθε καμοντας
ανθρωπους τιννσθον, οτις κ'επιορκν ομοσση,
υμεις μαρτυροι εστε, φυλασσετε δ'ορκια πιοστα.[2]

---

[1] A.S., VII., 17.

Ζευ κ·υδιστε. μεγιστε, και αθανατοι θεοι αλλοι.
οπποτεροι προτεροι υπερ δρκια πημπνειαν,
ωδη οφ' εγκεφαλος χαμαδις ρεοι, ως οδε οινος,
αυτων, και τεκεων, αλοχοι δ'αλλοισι μιγειεν.

[2] Iliad, III., 276-80, tr. Philipson.

In historic Greece we find Cirrah being razed to the ground by the Amphictyonic Council owing to a transgression of sacred law on her part and the following curse was pronounced:

"If any one transgress this, whether city or individual, or tribe, let him be accursed of Apollo and Artemis and Leto and Athenæ; neither may the offenders' land bear fruit, nor their wives bring forth children like unto their parents but monsters, nor their herds yield increase after their kind; and may they suffer confusion in war and trials and in councils, may they be exterminated themselves, and their houses and their race; and may they never sacrifice acceptably to Apollo or Artemis or Leto or Athenæ, nor receive their sacrifices at their hands."[1]

Similarly, "Roman treaties were deemed to be under the vigilant guardianship of the gods. Thus Rome had her *Jupiter Fidius*, as Greece had her Ζευς Πιστιος. Janus is said to have been the protector of alliances; his double face symbolising the two peoples united by the treaty of peace. The conception of *fides* and πιστις and ορκια is at the very foundation not only of ancient treaties in the strict sense but of the whole range of Hellenic and Roman international relationships. Thus in the treaty between Hannibal and Philip V of Macedon (215 B. C.) the oath was taken, says Polybius, in the presence of Zeus, Hore, and Apollo; of the god of the Carthaginians, Hercules and Lobus, of Ares, Triton, Poseidon: of the gods that accompany the army, and the sun, moon and earth, of rivers, harbours and waters....................of all the gods of war that are witnesses to the oath.[2] The first Roman treaty with Carthage affords an interesting example. The Commissioner (*paterpatratus*), writes Polybius, took a

---

[1] Æschines: Ctesiphon. (Philipson).

[2] Polybius, VII., 9.

stone in his hand and having taken the oath in the name of his country concluded with these words: 'If I abide by this oath may Jupiter bless me; but if I do otherwise in thought or act, may all others prosper in their countries under their laws, in their livelihood, and preserve their household goods and tombs; may I alone be cast out as this stone is now."[1] According to Martin[2] in China too, there were elaborate formalities in connection with the signing of a treaty including solemn confirmation by oath, mingling of the blood of the signatory parties in a cup of wine, laying their hands on the head of an ox to be sacrificed, and the usual imprecation. Thus in a treaty between the Prince of Cheng, and a coalition of princes who invaded his terrirtory, 544 B.C., after the preamble and the recital of the provisions, the conclusion was to this effect: "We engage to maintain inviolate the terms of the foregoing agreement. May the gods of the hills and the rivers, the spirits of former Emperors and Dukes, and the ancestors of our seven tribes and twelve states watch over its fulfilment. If any one prove unfaithful may the all-seeing gods smite him, so that his people shall forsake him, his life be lost and his posterity cut off."[3]

As however time rolled on, the need for ample guarantees for securing treaties besides "oath" arose and "securities" and "hostages" came to be demanded for a due observance of the terms.[4] **प्रतिभू:** is peace with a

---

[1] Polybius, III., 25.

[2] Martin, *cit.*, p. 73.

[3] Philipson.

[4] *Cf.* also Æneid, XII, 197-205.

> "haec eadem, Aenea, terrum-mare sidera juro
> Latonaeque genus duplex Ianumque bifrontem
> Vimque deum infernam et duri sacraria Ditis;
> audit haec genitor, qui foedera fulmine sandit.
> tango aras medios ignis et numina testor;

security—" ascetics engaged in penance," and " noble men " were offered as securities. The deeply religious nature of the Indians prompted them to offer ascetics engaged in penance as the most efficient means of keeping the plighted word. प्रतिग्रहः is peace made with hostages: they might be children, princesses or princes. Kautilya bursts forth in grim humour when he solemnly advises the conquering hero not to accept, if possible, princesses as hostages because they cause trouble to the receiver.

बन्धुमुख्यप्रग्रहः प्रतिग्रहः ; तस्मिन्यो दूष्यापत्यं वा ददाति सोऽतिसन्धत्ते । विपरीतोऽतिसन्धीयते । प्रतिग्रहग्रहणविश्वस्तस्य हि परः छिद्रेषु निरपेक्षः प्रहरति ।[1]

Kautilya's sage advice is confirmed by the experience of the Romans. With the beginning of the Empire, Rome frequently received women as hostages. In the case of some communities, says Suetonius, " Augustus required a new kind of hostage, *viz.*, women, as he had found from experience that they cared little for men when thus delivered."

---

nulla dies pacem hanc Italis nec foedera rumpet,
quo res cumque cadent; nec me visulla volentem
avertet, non si tellurem effundatin undas
diluvio miscens caelumque in Tartara solvat."

Thus Latinus looking towards the sky and extending his hands to heaven says: " By these same I swear. O Aeneas, by the Earth, sea, sky, and the twin brood of Latona and Janus the double facing, and the might of nether gods and grim Pluto's Shrine; this let our Father hear, who seals treaties with his thunderbolt. I touch the altars, I take to witness the fires and the gods between us; no time shall break this peace and truce in Italy: howsoever fortune fall; nor shall any force turn my will aside, not if it dissolve land into water in turmoil of deluge, nor melt in heaven."—Philipson.

[1] *Cf.* the "*Chinabhuktis.*"

" शपथातिक्रमे महतां तपस्विनां मुख्यानां वा प्रातिभाव्यबन्धः प्रतिभूः ।"

A. S., VII., 17.

Suetonius: Augustus 21 "...... novum genus obsidum, feminas, exigere temptaverit, quod negligore marum pignera sentiebat."

Thus, the institution of hostages obtained universally among nations of antiquity and the practice continued down to comparatively recent times; we hear of it in Europe even so late as the year 1748, when two English peers were sent to Paris as pledges for the fulfilment of the treaty of Aix-la-Chapelle.

We have seen the various classifications of treaties, we have examined the various guarantees for peace; now comes the question to the forefront, how far were treaties binding? The international conscience of civilised world has raised the question in an acute form during recent times. Treaties, says Hall, are entered into between parties as binding. "Treaties," says Sir F. E. Smith, "form the contract law of states, and it is in dealing with their enforcement and deviation that International Law conspicuously fails." He observes the distinction between municipal law and International Law specially on the questions of specific performance of a contract: "whereas municipal law will not hold valid a contract obtained by force, many of the most important treaties of the world are the result of the exercise of force, or the threat of it, upon a nation which has no alternative but surrender. To treat force, therefore, as invalidating a treaty would be to strike at the conclusion of a war."[1] And yet, fraud vitiates agreements of all kinds and Phillimore gives an illustration of duress nullifying an engagement: "The resignation of the crown and kingdom, extorted by Napoleon from Ferdinand VII at Bayonne, whither he had decoyed the monarch and his family was clearly—the duress and the condition of the party abdicating being considered—invalid; but the resignation of Napoleon at Fontainebleau was not extorted by treachery or duress, but was the consequence of defeat in open

---

[1] F. E. Smith: International Law, p. 142.

and legitimate war."[1] This view if pushed to extremes would justify the treaty executed by the German Imperial administration at Brest Litovsk in the year 1917. Woolsey however, takes a different standpoint and observes: "A combination to commit injustice, for example, to conquer and appropriate an independent country, as Poland, is a crime which no formalities of treaty can sanction. This rule it is true, is not one of much political importance or of practical application to the concerns of nations beforehand, for most of the iniquities of nations are varnished over by some justifying plea and the only tribunal in the case is the moral indignation of mankind, while after the crime has triumphed mankind accepts the new order of things rather than have a state of perpetual war." Political philosophers of the German school on the other hand, like Trietsche and Nietsche are of opinion, that peace ought to be maintained—at any rate peace forced on a nation—only so long as the vanquished state does not recoup sufficient strength to retaliate. The bloody battle of Jena and the humiliating terms of peace imposed upon the Germans by Napoleon, engendered a feeling of distrust for treaties in the minds of the German political thinkers of the last century.

Treaties of guarantees, which the European family of nations delights in, 'while imposing them on Belgium or Switzerland or the dismembered Ottoman Empire, do not seem to have been scrupulously observed by the members themselves. Thus in 1871, when the plenipotentiaries assembled were clamouring for the sanctity of international agreements, the powers were engaged in acquiescing in a flagrant violation of the Treaty of Paris in 1856, according to which Russia was forbidden to maintain a fleet in the Black Sea. Then again, Bosnia and

---

[1] Phillimore: Commentaries upon Int. Law, II., § 49.

Herzegovina were annexed by the late "Dual Empire" in violation of the Treaty of Berlin, 1878. In 1831, the neutrality of Belgium was guaranteed; it was violated by one of the contracting parties, *viz.*, Germany in 1914; in 1856, the Convention of Paris between Great Britain and France and Austria ensured the independence and integrity of the Ottoman Empire; shortly after, bankruptcy and lawlessness in Egypt evoked English interference, English protectorate and lastly annexation. The conclusion of the last great European War will probably soon see the dismemberment of the Turkish Empire by two of the contracting powers, and the Khalifat day in India will be observed in vain.

This somewhat long preamble is necessary to explain the peculiar theory of peace propounded by the writers of the Arthasastras in Ancient India. They realised full well the truth of the remark शमव्यायामौ योगक्षेमयोर्योनिः[1] and yet the centralisation and deification of the monarchy led them to promulgate the theory of expediency. To an astute politician like Kautilya, who helped the overthrow of the Nanda dynasty, the installation of the Mauryya Emperors and the acquisition of their vast empire, restlessness appeared to be the only means of success and he therefore upheld the theory of the "good old rule, the simple plan:" "whoever is rising in power, may break an agreement of peace"[2] and "a powerless king should behave as a conquered king" अशक्तो दण्डोपनतवद्वर्त्तेत[3] and there cannot be a greater evil to a king than alliance with a considerable power—महादोषो हि विशिष्टबलसमागमो राज्ञामन्यत्रारिविगृहीतात्।[4] So a king according to him, was to maintain peace only under certain circumstances.

[1] Arthasastra, VI., 2.

[2] *Ibid*, VII., 17.

[3] *Ibid*, VII., 2.

[4] *Ibid.*

Like the politicians and diplomats of modern Europe the writer of the Arthasastras recommended "an armed" peace. Thus says Kautilya:

यदिवा पश्येत्—सन्धौ स्थितो महाफलैः स्वकर्मभिः परकर्माण्युपहनिष्यामि ; महाफलानि वा स्वकर्माण्युपभोक्ष्ये ; परकर्माणिवा ; सन्धिविश्वासेनवा योगोपनिषत्प्रणिधिभिः परकर्माण्युपहनिष्यामि ; सुखं वा सानुग्रहपरिहारसौकर्यफललाभभूयस्त्वेन स्वकर्म्मणा परकर्म्मयोगावहजनमास्रावयिष्यामि ; बलिनाऽतिमात्रेण वा संहितः परः स्वकर्म्मोपघातं प्राप्स्यति ; येनवा विगृहीतो मया सन्धत्ते, तेन अस्य विग्रहं दीर्घं करिष्यामि ; मया वा संहितस्य मद्द्वेषिणो जनपदं पीड़यिष्यति ; परोपहतो वाऽस्य जनपदो मामागमिष्यति ; ततः कर्म्मसु वृद्धिं प्राप्स्यामि ; विपन्नकर्म्मारम्भो वा विषमस्थः परः कर्म्मसु न मे विक्रमेत ; परतः प्रवृत्तकर्म्मारम्भो वा ताभ्यां संहितः कर्म्मसु वृद्धिं प्राप्स्यामि ; शत्रुप्रतिबद्धं वा शत्रुणा सन्धिं कृत्वा मण्डलं भेत्स्यामि ; भिन्नमवाप्स्यामि ; दण्डानुग्रहेण वा शत्रुमुपगृह्य मण्डललिप्सायां विद्वेषं ग्राहयिष्यामि ; विद्विष्टं तेनैव घातयिष्यामि "इति सन्धिना वृद्धिमातिष्ठेत् ॥"[1] This is the voice of

---

[1] A. S., VII. 1. Or if a king thinks, "that keeping the agreement of peace I can undertake productive works of considerable importance and destroy at the same time those of the enemy; or apart from enjoying the results of my own works, I shall also enjoy those of my enemy in virtue of the agreement of peace; or I can destroy the works of my enemy by employing spies and other secret means; or by holding out such inducements as a happy dwelling, rewards, remission of taxes, little work and large profits and wages, I can empty my enemy's country of its population with which he has been able to carry out his own works; or being allied with a king of considerable power my enemy will have his own works destroyed; or I can prolong my enemy's hostility with another King whose threats have driven my enemy to seek my protection; or being allied with me my enemy can harass the country of another king who hates me; or oppressed by another king, the subjects of my enemy will immigrate into my country, and I can therefore achieve the results of my own works very easily; or being in a precarious condition due to the destruction of his works my enemy will not be so powerful as to attack me; or by exploiting my own resources in alliance with any two kings, I can augment my resources; or if a circle of states is formed by my enemy as one of its members, I can divide them and combine with others; or by threats or favour, I can catch hold of my enemy and when he desires to be a member of my own circle of states, I can make him incur the displeasure of other members and fall a victim to their own fury"—if a king thinks thus, then he may increase his resources by keeping peace."—Shama Sastri's translation, p. 329.

political expediency prompting a state to the adoption of only one principle, *viz.*, satisfaction of state-interest.[1] Thus, it will be observed that all the activities of the state are subordinated to its supreme interests. Self-improvement, the adoption of an attitude of benevolent neutrality, all questions of naturalisation, immigration, and emigration, the formation of alliances, the preservation of the balance of power are guided by the dominating and all-absorbing passion of self-interest. This theory of peace has been defined by Sukracharyya very briefly :[2]

सन्धिश्चातिबले युद्धं साम्ये यानन्तु दुर्ब्बले ।
सुहृद्भिराश्रयः स्थानं दुर्गाभिभजनं द्विधा ॥
बलिना सह सन्ध्याय भये साधारणे यदि ।
आत्मानं गोपयेत् कालेवह्वमित्रेषु बुद्धिमान् ॥

The value of alliances from the "utilitarian" point of view is very great and a king should "like a bamboo remain surrounded by clusters."

सङ्घातवान् यथा वेणुर्निविड़ैः कण्टकैर्वृतः ।
नशक्यते समुच्छेत्तुं वेणुः सङ्घातवांस्तथा ॥[3]

"Therefore, being attacked by a powerful monarch, a ruler of men having no other remedy should seek peace, delaying as much as possible."[4]

Thus equality of status came to be recognized as the most stable basis of "peace with honour," and a king desiring prosperity was to conclude peace with his equals because "the clash between two unbaked jars destroys both of them."

---

1 *Vide ante.*

बलीयसाभियुक्तस्तु नृपोऽनन्यप्रतिक्रियः ।
आपन्नः सन्धिमन्विच्छेत्कुर्व्वाणः कालयापनाम् ॥ Kam., IX., 1.

2 Peace should be made with the very powerful, war with the equal and expedition against the weak; but to friends should be granted refuge as well as residence within the forts.—Sarkar.

4 Sukra, IV., vii., 244.

"नत्सम्प्रहृष्टेरतिहृष्टिकामः
समेन सन्धानमिहोपगच्छेत् ।
अपक्वयोर्व्वा घटयोरवश्य
मन्योन्यभेदो समसन्निपातः ॥"[1]

"A weak king," thus ran the advice of Kamandaka, "should patiently bear the thrashing of the enemy, like a tortoise contracting within its shell when beaten; but when the right time comes, the intelligent king should behave like a crooked serpent."

अपरिभ्रश्यमानं हि क्रमप्राप्ते मृगेन्द्रवत् ॥
कौर्म्मसङ्कोचमास्थाय प्रहारमपि मर्षयेत् ।
काले प्राप्तेतु मतिमानुत्तिष्ठेत् क्रूरसर्पवत् ॥[2]

It was this principle of expediency wh ich ind uced Manu to dictate as follows :

नित्यमुद्यतदण्डः स्यान्नित्यं विवृतपौरुषः ।
नित्यं संवृतसंव्वार्य्यो नित्यं छिद्रानुसार्य्यरेः ॥
नित्यमुद्यतदण्डस्य कृत्स्नमुद्विजते जगत् ।
तस्मात् सर्व्वाणि भूतानि दण्डेनैव प्रसाधयेत् ॥[3]

In all states of antiquity, in the inevitable contest between justice and expediency, the welfare of the state was regarded as the primary consideration of every citizen and the ideas of writers of the Arthasastras agreed with those of Livy who looked upon honour as subservient to utility—*cui utilis quam honesti cura erat.* Law to them, was merely a creature of circumstance and necessity.

Honesta lex est temporis necessitas
Necessitas dat legem, non ipsa accipit.[4]

---

[1] Kam., IX., 60.

[2] Kam., X., 34-35.

[3] Let him be ever ready to strike, his prowess constantly displayed, and his secrets constantly concealed, and let him constantly explore the weaknesses of his foe. Of him who is always ready to strike, the whole world stands in awe; let him therefore make all creatures subject to himself even by the employment of force —Manu, VII., 102-03.

[4] Publilius Syras (45 B.C.) Sententiae.

The keen struggle between justice and expediency was felt many a time by the Greeks. Thus, the Corinthian envoys on the eve of the Peloponnesian War reminded the Athenians of the apparent harmony between the two extremes :[1] "Do not say to yourselves," they said, "that one thing is just but that in the event of war another thing is expedient ; for the true path of expediency is the path of right." Thus did the Athenians enunciate the general policy of Athens before Hermocrates of Syracuse : "In each case we must make friends or enemies, according to circumstances and here our interest requires, not that we should weaken our friends, but that our friends should be too strong for our enemies. Do not mistrust us. In Hellas we act upon the same principles, managing our allies as our interest requires in their several cases."[2] Of the view of the supremacy of state interest, and of the practice of subordinating everything else thereto, the Spartans were the most thorough, consistent and uncompromising advocates. Lysander's preference for expediency and strategem to justice and openness is well known. He indeed laughed at those who said that the race of Heracles ought not to make wars by strategem, saying : "when the lion's skin will not protect us, we must sew the fox's skin to it."

οπου γαρ η λεοντημη εφικνειται, πρθσπραητεον ε'κει την αλωπενην.[3]

---

[1] Thuc., I., 78 : *καιμη νομιοη δικαια μεν ταδε λεγεσθαι ξυμφορα δε, ει πολεμησει, αλλα το τε γαρξυμφερον εν ω αν τις ελαχιστα αμαρτανη μαλιστα ετεται...... το γαρ μη αδικειν τους ομοιους εχυρωτερα δυναμις η τω αυτικα φανερω επαρθεντας δια κινδυνωντο πλεον εχειν.*

[2] Thuc., VI., 85 : *προς εκαστα δε δει η εχθρον η φιλον μετα καιρου γιγνεσθαι και ημας τουτο ωφελει ευεθαδε, ουκ ην τους φιλους κακωσωμεν, αλλ ην οι εχθροι δια των των φιλων αδυνατοι ωσσιν απιστεον δεου χρη και γαρ τους εκει ξυμμαχους ων εκαστοι χρησιμοι εξηγουμεθα.........*

[3] Plut. : Lysander, 7.

CHAPTER VII

WAR : CHARACTER : GROUNDS

It has been asserted and re-iterated by admirers of modern International Law—conversant with the histories of Rome and Greece—that the ancients lived amidst the ceaseless turmoil of war, that an interminable mutual hostility of nations was their normal and necessary condition, and they held every alien to be essentially and inevitably an ἐχθρός or *hostis*, in the sense of a political or natural adversary. Now, as it will be shown in this chapter, war did not form the normal condition of existence so far as at least the three great Aryan peoples of antiquity were concerned, *viz.*, the ancient Indians, the Greeks and the Romans. According to the Greeks and the Romans, war was admittedly their frequent condition but certain well-defined causes regularized military operations; while in the case of ancient India, of the six forms of policy, conciliation, gift and separation were given preference to war even in a regular form.

"'If thy endeavours after peace fail, then mayest thou engage in battle,' such was the advice of the dying Bhisma to Yudhisthir. 'The victory that one acquires by battle is very inferior.'[1] Therefore the collision of battle is not at all desirable as long as it can be avoided. The policy of conciliation, of producing disunion and making

---

[1] संहत्य महतीं सेनां चतुरङ्गां युधिष्ठिर ।
साम्नैव वर्त्तयेः पूर्व्वं प्रयतेथास्ततो युधि ॥
जघन्य एष विजयो यद्युद्धं सामभाषणं ।
याहच्छिको युधि जयो दैवेनेति विचारणम् ।

Sant., CII., 16-17.

gifts should first be tried; battle, it is said, should come after these"[1]

The Manu Samhita also repeats the same sentiments. A king should first try to conquer his foes by conciliation, by gift and by causing dissension if possible: if all these fail then and then only should he wage war.

साम्नादानेन भेदेन समस्तैरथवा पृथक् ।
विजेतुं प्रयतेतारीन् न युद्धेन कदाचन ॥[2]

* * * *

त्रयाणामप्युपायानां पूर्व्वोक्तानामसंभवे ।
तथा युध्येत संयत्तो विजयेत रिपून् यथा ॥[2]

The Arthasastras were great advocates of the policy of state-interest and yet they looked upon the establishment and continuation of peace as the only means of achieving national progress and national prosperity.[3] Even when the advantages of peace and war are equal one should prefer peace, for war causes loss of power and wealth and is troublesome and sinful.[4] A solvent treasury and sage advice, declared Kamandaka, were much better expedients than mere display of power; he therefore recommended lavish use of gifts.

चतुरङ्गबलं मुक्त्वा कोषो मन्त्रश्च युध्यते ।
तत् साधुमन्त्रो मन्त्रेण कोषेण च जयेदरीन् ॥
साम दानञ्च दण्डश्च भेदश्चेति चतुष्टयम् ।
मायोपेक्षेन्द्रजालं च सप्तोपायाः प्रकीर्त्तिताः ॥[5]

---

[1] सन्निपातो न मन्तव्यः शक्ये सति कथञ्चन ।

सान्त्वभेदप्रदानानां युद्धमुत्तरमुच्यते ॥

Mahabharata-Santi-Raj, CII., 22.

[2] Manu, VII., 198.

[3] *Ibid*, VII., 200.

[4] Arthasastra, VII., 12.

सन्धि विग्रहयोस्तुल्यायां वृद्धौ सन्धिमुपेयात् । विग्रहे हि क्षयव्ययप्रवासप्रत्यवाया भवन्ति—

[5] Kamandaka, XVII., 2-3.

Conciliations and gifts are of five kinds while there were three forms of the policy of separation. 'The enumeration of services rendered mutually, high praise of the deeds of the enemy, establishment of relationships, display of majesty as well as a peaceful declaration of allegiance—these are the five sorts of conciliation.' Gift of wealth, exchange of commodities, acquiescence in seizure, gift of valuable things and remission of dues were regarded as the various kinds of "gifts." Dissension could be caused by alienation, by causing rivalry and by the expression of threats. Sukracharyya is the great exponent of, and a firm believer in, the efficacy of the power of separation and he held that separation was the best of all methods or policies of work.[1] Victory in war was regarded as uncertain and war was therefore to be avoided as long as possible from the utilitarian point of view:[2] that was the opinion of the writers of the Arthasastras while the Dharmasastras advised abstention from hostilities from a moral point of view.

Similarly, in the histories of Greece and Rome we find expressions of pacific intention of states amidst the prevailing clash of arms. Thus Pericles in his "Funeral Orations" gave vent to his pacific intentions and wanted to make peaceful Athens the "Schoolmistress" of Hellas. Thus Aristophanes[3] supplicated the gods to abolish the arbitrament of the sword, and Euripides[4] advised avoidance of war as inconsistent with wisdom; though thoroughly

---

[1] Sukra, IV., vii.

[2] Sukra, IV., vii., 189: "शत्रु संसाधनोपायो नान्य: सुबलभिदत: "

सुहृज्जनं तथा राज्यमात्मानं कीर्त्तिमेवच ।

युधि सन्देहदोलास्थं को हि कूर्य्याद बालिश: ॥

Kam., IX., 75.

[3] Aves, 1591.

[4] "It behoves him therefore whoever is wise, to avoid war, but if it come to this, it is no crown of dishonour to die nobly for one's city, but to die ignobly is shameful."—Troad.

imbued with purely chivalrous feelings, he did not advocate ignoble or dishonourable death.

> φευγειν μεν ουν χρηπολεμου, οστισευ φρονει
> ει δες τοδ ελθοι, στεφανος ουκ αισχρος πολει
> καλως ολεσθαι μη καλως δε δυσκλεες.

The Roman writers were no less vehement in their denunciation of wars and they agreed with Aristotle in regarding peace as the ultimate goal of all wars (τελοςγαρ ειρηνημεν πολεμου). Thus Silius Italicus emphasizes that peace is the best of all things given to mankind, and that one peace is better than innumerable triumphs.

> Pax optima rerum
> quas homini novisse datum est; pax una triumphis
> innumeris potior.

"Peace with justice and honour," so declares Polybius,[1] "is the noblest and the most advantageous thing in the world; when joined with disgrace and contemptible cowardice, it is the basest and the most disastrous." Hence sang Pindar:

> το κοινον τις αστων εν ευδια τι θεις
> ερευνασατω μεγαλανορος ησυχιας το φαιδρον φαος

> "A quiet haven for the ship of the state
> Should be the patriot's aim,
> And smiling peace to small and great
> That brings no shame."[2]

The various definitions of "war" given by the writers of the Arthasastras prove that they regarded war not as a condition but as a result of what Logicians regard as a series of causes. Kautilya defined war as an "offensive operation."[3] War was defined by Sukracharyya as (*i*) the affair of two parties, (*ii*) having inimical relations

[1] IV., 31.

[2] Odes, Philipson.

[3] Arthasastra, Bk. VII., I.

with each other, (*iii*) undertaken by means of arms, (*iv*) with the ulterior object of satisfying their rival interests :

आविभ्रतोः शत्रुभावमुभयोः संयतात्मनोः ।
अस्त्राद्यैः स्वार्थसिद्ध्यर्थं व्यापारो युद्धमुच्यते ॥[1]

The Agni Purana defines war " as the direct result of injuries done to each other by two hostile monarchs."[2] If we combine the essential ingredients then it will be seen, that the authors of the Arthasastras did not in any way regard warfare as a necessary consequence of existence and that there was probably the nearest approach to the theory of modern International Law that war is an affair between states. It will also be seen later, that the distinction between combatants and non-combatants—a distinction scarcely recognized by international custom of antiquity—was fully recognized and acted upon in ancient India.[3]

A declaration of war is a formal notification on the part of a state that it considers itself at war with another state to which a notification is sent. A universal rule of declaration, preceding commencement of hostilities was the general custom of antiquity. Thus, in ancient India all the great wars in the Epics were begun after declaration. Declarations of war were generally made through the *Dutas*, as for example, Srikrishna, as an ambassador of the Pandavas, delivered his *ultimatum* to the *Kauravas*: in historical times this good old rule was strictly followed, so that issue of

[1] Sukra, IV., vii., 220.
[2] Agni, CCXL., 15, p. 860, tr.
[3] *Cf.* also Kamandaka, X., 1 :

अमर्षोपगृहीतानां मन्युसन्तप्तचेतसां ।
परस्परापकारेण पुंसां भवतिविग्रहः ॥

ultimatums (प्रताप)[1] and breaking of treaties (समाधिमोक्ष:) have been mentioned by Kautilya, as the functions of an envoy or *Duta*. Such declarations took the form of an oral delivery of message by the delivery of *Sasana* or royal writ. "Writs," says Kautilya, "are of great importance, in as much as treaties and *ultimata* depend upon writs."[2] Hence, a person possessing the qualifications of a minister, who knows very well the customs and usages of the country, who is smart in composition, whose handwriting is legible and who is sharp in reading should be appointed a *lekhaka*.

शासन प्रधानाहिराजान: तन्मूलत्वात् सन्धिविग्रहयो:[1]। तस्मादमात्य-सम्पदोपेत: सर्व्वसमय विदाशुग्रन्यश्चार्वक्षरो लेखवाचनसमर्थो लेखक: स्यात् ॥

In Chapter IV of Book VII, Kautilya deals with Neutrality *after proclaiming war* (विगृह्यासनं) and marching after *proclaiming* war (विगृह्ययानं). He states also therein the circumstances under which a king may keep quiet after *proclaiming* war. We observe the triumph of the Kautilyan theory of expediency when we find Kautilya counselling princes 'gaining in strength after proclaiming war,' to march against a helpless enemy:

"विगृह्यासनहेतुभिरभ्युच्चित: सर्व्वसन्दोहवर्जं विगृह्य यायात्"[3]

One thing however remains clear : whether a king desires to overpower a weak neighbour, whether he launches war upon a state for the preservation of the balance of

---

[1] प्रेषणंसन्धिपालत्वं प्रतापो मित्रसंग्रह: ।

*   *   *   *

*   *   *   *

समाधिमोक्षो दूतस्य कर्म्मयोगस्यचाश्रय: ।—A.S., I., 16.

Cf. also Kam., XII., 8:

"उद्यतेष्वपि शस्त्रेषु यथोक्तं शासनं वदेत्"

[2] Arthasastra, II., 10.

[3] Arthasastra, VII., 4.

power, or whether he fights in self-defence, proclamation of war should precede commencement of hostilities. Further on, in Kautilya's definition of "धर्म्मयुद्ध" and "कूटयुद्ध"[1] surprise attack does not form one of the constituent elements, so that we can come to the conclusion that war must have been preceded by a declaration of hostilities. The Greeks and the Romans were also very strict in regard to the observance of certain formalities connected with the declaration of war. But declaration was dispensed with in cases of wars of self-defence[2] as well as in cases of wars against an improperly organised people, or against a nation deprived of independence and freedom, on the ground that legal equality could not obtain in the absence of juridical personality.[3] The Spartans who were notorious for their military proclivities did not care to observe such previous notification. Thus, Pausanias says in reference to their designs on Messenia that they neither declared war by herald, nor openly renounced their friendship. But when Sparta was in her turn attacked by Pyrrhus long afterwards without any previous declaration, the Spartan envoys remonstrated with him and his reply was: "We know well that neither do you Spartans tell any one beforehand what you mean to do."[4]

---

1 Arthasastra, VII., 6:

प्रकाशयुद्धं निर्द्दिष्टौ देशे कालेच विक्रमः।
विभीषणमवस्कन्दः प्रमादव्यसनार्दनम् ॥
एकत्र त्यागघातौ च कूटयुद्धस्य मातृका।
योगभूतौपजापार्थं तुष्णीं युद्धस्य लक्षणम् ॥

but see later; Kautilya distinguishes between धर्म्मयुद्ध and कूटयुद्ध according as hostilities follow declaration of war or not.

2 *Cf.* Livy: XXXVI., 3.

3 Dig., XXII., 15. 7. 1.

4 *προπεμψαντες κηρυκα προτερον πολεμον προερουντα* ....

The principle of public declaration of war before actual commencement of hostilities was fully recognised by Greece and Rome. Thus, Herodotus refers to the Greek custom of declaring war before the beginning of belligerent operations—επεαν γαρ αλληλοισι πολεμον προειπωσι...... μαχονται. So, on the failure of arbitration between the Corcyraeans and the Corinthians on the eve of the Peloponnesian war, a herald was despatched to the enemy to proclaim that a state of war existed between the two countries.[1] In Rome, the *Jus fetiale* consisted of certain rules and ceremonies or modes of procedure for declarations of war and ratifications of treaties of peace which were of great antiquity and were intended to satisfy the religious scruples and the sensitive "legal-conscience" of the Romans.

There seems to be a great difference of opinion among writers of "modern" International Law as to whether declaration of war is at all necessary. The English and the American publicists have held the view that the date of the first outbreak of hostilities furnishes a better criterion for the commencement of a war than the date of the formal declaration. Their view is perhaps best expressed by Hall:[2]

"An act of hostility, unless it be done in the urgency of self-preservation, or by way of special reprisal, is in itself a full declaration of intention: any sort of previous declaration therefore is an empty formality, unless an enemy must be given time and opportunity to put himself in a state of defence, and it is needless to say that no one asserts such quixotism to be obligatory." The very magnitude of the British empire demands a quick beginning as a condition precedent to success, and

---

[1] See also *Eclogues*. Thucydides, I., 29.

[2] Hall: Sixth Ed., p. 370.

hence the English publicists do not favour an open declaration before war is actually begun. General Maurice of the British army[1] found less than ten cases out of 118 examined, of declarations prior to hostilities between 1700 and 1872.

The majority of the continental jurists have insisted upon the utility or necessity of declaration. Japanese custom does not conform to the practice of beginning war with a declaration. Thus, the Chino-Japanese war began with the capture of the Chinese transport *Koshung*[2] by a Japanese Cruiser. Considerable controversy was also roused by the Russian charge of treachery against the Japanese because of the latter's attack on the Russian fleet at Chemulpo and at Port Arthur two days prior to Japan's declaration of war against Russia.[3] The question was attempted to be set at rest by the second Hague Peace Conference which went back to antiquity and laid down the rule that hostilities between contracting powers "must not commence without previous and explicit warning, in the form either of a declaration of war with the reasons assigned for it or of an ultimatum with conditional declaration of war."[4] This rule seems to have been observed in general by the belligerent powers during the last great European and a practice of universal application in antiquity seems to have been translated for modern acceptance.

Wars have been due to various and manifold causes. They are partly psychological, social, economic or political in origin. "They have their root in human nature, in the passions, appetites, aversions and ambitions of mankind; and in the economic, political, or social conditions

---

[1] Hostilities without Declaration, 1883.

[2] Takahashi: International Law applied to the Russo-Japanese War, 23; 602.

[3] See also Lawrence: War and Neutrality in the Far East.

[4] Higgins: Hague Peace Conference, 198-99.

under which men seek for the means of existence and enjoyment. On the one hand, we have to reckon with certain human factors, such as hunger, greed, national jealousy, racial aversion, love of glory or national vanity, and a desire to gratify these passions: and on the other hand, man is often confronted with conditions in his physical, political and social environment which make it difficult to gratify these desires without a resort to violence."[1]

"The causes which usually give rise to a war and the affronts which are usually amended through the arbitration of the sword, are, says the Agnipurana,[2] (*i*) the stealing away of a wife,[3] (*ii*) encroachment upon the capital, (*iii*) the territory, (*iv*) the kingdom, (*v*) or the sovereign right of a king by his adversary, (*vi*) pride, (*vii*) over-sensitiveness as to the point of honour, (*viii*) loss of fortune, (*ix*) humiliation suffered by an ally or a friendly monarch, (*x*) the death of an ally, (*xi*) the accretion to the domain of a foreign prince and a disturbance of the balance of power[4] among the monarchs of a circle."[5]

Almost the same ideas have been expressed by Kamandaka—only intervention on moral grounds being considered by him as an additional ground for war:

आत्मनोऽभ्युदयाकाङ्क्षी पीड्यमानः परेण वा ।
देशकालबलोपेतः प्रारभेत हि विग्रहम् ॥

---

[1] New York Independent, Vol. 57, 1036.

[2] Ag., CCXL.

[3] *E.g.*, the wars between Rama and Ravana; the war of Rome with Veii and Lars Porsena.

[4] The theory of the *Mandala*.

[5] Wars were frequently undertaken by the Romans for offences caused against ambassadors and for refusal to surrender or receive an ambassador. Thus, the Romans early in their career, declared war against Veii for maltreatment of Roman ambassadors. A tribune reproached the King of the Veientians with these words: "Is this the breaker of human treaties, the violator of the law of Nations? This victim will I now slay and I will offer him up to the shades of the ambassadors."—Livy: IV., 58.

राज्यस्त्रीस्थानदेशानां यानस्य च धनस्य च ।
अपहारो मदो मानः पीड़ा वैषयिकी तथा ॥
ज्ञानार्थधर्म्मशक्तीनां विघातो दैवमेव च ।
मित्रार्थं चापमानश्च तथा वन्धुविनाशनम् ॥
भूतानुग्रहविच्छेदस्तथा मण्डलदूषणम् ।
एकार्थाभिनिवेशित्वमिति विग्रहयोनयः ॥[1]

In the above list of 'causes' or occasions for war we miss (*i*) wars for the refusal of extradition, (*ii*) wars of religion and (*iii*) wars for offences against diplomatic agents. Probably wars of religion did not disturb the peace of India at such an early period as that of Kamandaka, or perhaps civil wars, as with the Romans, were not reckoned as wars by the Indians.

Wars were divided into various classes according either to (*i*) the weapons used or (*ii*) the methods employed. Sukracharyya divided wars into (1) दैविक, (2) आसुर and (3) मानुष, according to the weapons used. The *daivika* warfare is that in which मन्त्र was used; the आसुर is that in which mechanical instruments were used; and human warfare is that in which *Sastras* and hands were used.

मन्त्रास्त्रैर्दैविकं युद्धं नालाद्यस्त्रैस्तथाऽसुरम् ।
शस्त्रबाहुसमुत्थन्तु मानवं युद्धमीरितम् ॥[2]

Kautilya divided battles into (*i*) open battle, (*ii*) treacherous battle, and (*iii*) silent battle, according to the means employed.

"विक्रमस्य प्रकाशयुद्धं, कूटयुद्धं, तुष्णीं युद्धमिति ।"[3]

Open, treacherous and silent battles have further been defined thus: [4]

प्रकाशयुद्धं निर्द्दिष्टो देशे कालेच विक्रमः ।
विभीषणमवस्कन्दः प्रमादव्यसनार्दनम् ॥

[1] Kam., X., 2-6.
[2] Sukra, IV., vii., 221.
[3] Arthasastra, VII., 6.
[4] *Ibid*, VII., 6.

एकत्र त्यागघातौ च कूटयुद्धस्य मातृका ।
योगभूमौपजापार्थं तुष्णीं युद्धस्य लक्षणम् ॥

When a battle is fought in daylight and in some locality, it is termed an "open battle"; bribing a portion of the army and destroying another portion is one of the forms of treacherous fight, while intrigue is the essence of a "silent battle" and desperate attempts were made to win over the chief officers of the enemy by bribery and intrigue. A weak king, according to the precepts of the Arthasastras, should wage both "treacherous" and "silent wars" against a powerful enemy. Silent battles could be started without previous declaration of hostile intention, but it will be evident from a careful perusal of Kautilya that silent battles were fought by the employment of spies. They are not battles at all in the modern acceptance of the term but should rather be regarded as a means of causing dissension in enemy's ranks by secret agencies—a method which has proved so very successful during the last great European war both in Russia as well as in Germany.

Indra, one of the traditional authors of the Arthasastra, divided wars into four classes: (*i*) wars caused by the invasion of one's territory, (*ii*) wars caused by something done by others prejudicial to the exercise of the regal powers, (*iii*) wars resulting from some dispute about boundaries, and (*iv*) wars caused by some disturbance in the *Mandala*.

जातं भूम्युपरोधेन तथा शक्तिविघातजं ॥
भूम्यनन्तरजातं तु मण्डलक्षोभजन्तथा ।
चतुर्विधं वैरजातं बहु दन्तीसुतोऽब्रवीत् ॥[1]

Kamandaka[2] divides wars into sixteen classes according to their results, their causes and the parties engaged.

[1] Kam., X., 16-17. [2] *Ibid*, X., 18-22.

His division does not seem to have a scientific basis at all.

"किञ्चित्फलं निष्फलञ्च सन्दिग्ध फलमेव च ।
तदात्वे दोषजननमायत्वाञ्चैव निष्फलम् ॥
अपरिज्ञातवीर्य्येण दुष्टेन स्तम्भितोऽपि वा ।
परार्थं स्त्रीनिमित्तञ्च दीर्घकालं द्विजोत्तमैः ॥
अकाले दैवयुक्तेन वलोद्धृतसखेन च ।
तदात्वे फलसंयुक्तमायत्यां फलवर्जितम् ॥
आयत्यां फलसंयुक्तं तदात्वे निष्फलं तथा ।
इतीमं षोड़शविधं नकुर्य्यादेव विग्रहम् ॥"

Sukracharyya draws a distinction between युद्ध and कलह with reference to the non-hostile intercourse between states. The cause of "कलह" or quarrel or contention is the exclusive demand for the same thing. When there is no other remedy, says he, war or *Vigraha* should be undertaken.

एकार्थाभिनिवेशित्वं कारणं कलहस्य वा ।
उपायान्तर नाशे तु ततो विग्रहमाचरेत् ॥ [1]

From the above sloka it is clear that कलह meant hostile operations stopping short of actual warfare. In a previous passage also, Sukracharyya while enumerating

---

[1] "War against illustrious Brahmans" is futile because all the ब्राह्मण had ब्रह्मतेज। That seems to be the view of Kamandaka. Sukracharyya on the other hand, is not afraid of a fight with the Brahmans; and when they take up arms, enemy character should be extended to them: "The Brahmana who appears with a murderous intent is as good as a Sudra." "There can be no sin in killing one who comes with a murderous intent." Then again: "The sin of killing a Brahmana does not touch the man who treats like a Kshattriya and kills the Brahmana who fights with arms in hand and does not leave the battlefield." Sukracharyya observes further: "When again the Kshattriyas have become effeminate and the people are being oppressed by the lower orders of men, the Brahmanas should fight and extirpate them."—Sukra IV., vii., 254.

the grounds of what we now call intervention on moral grounds says—

"विग्रहः स च विज्ञेयो ह्यन्यस्य कलहः स्मृतं।"[1]

Therefore, such hostile operations might assume various shapes and did certainly include "reprisals" as we understand it from a passage in the Arthasastra of Kautilya.[2]

समस्चेन्न सन्धिमिच्छेत्, यावन्मात्रमपकुर्य्यात्तावन्मात्रमस्य प्रत्यपकूर्य्यात्। तेजोहि सन्धानकारणं ; नातप्तं लौहं लौहेन सन्धत्त इति ॥

"When a king of equal power does not like peace, then the same amount of vexation as his opponent has received at his hands should be given to him in return; for it is power that brings about peace between two kings; no piece of iron that is not made red-hot will combine with another piece of iron."

These then were the general characteristics of war in ancient India. The Epics and the Dharmasastras would not recognise any kind of war which violated the strict rules of *Dharmajuddha* and this principle has been laid down over and over again by the great Epics, the Ramayana and the Mahabharata. It will be seen in the next chapter, that humanitarianism raised the laws of warfare in ancient India to a very high level, so that the distance of centuries vanishes in the mist of time. If humanitarianism therefore raised the tone of interstatal relations and international usage, chivalry also did not fail to discharge its task in ennobling the ideal of warfare

[1] Sukra, IV., vii., 252.

प्रहीनबलमित्रन्तु दुर्गस्थं शत्रुमागतम्।
अत्यन्तविषयासक्तं प्रजाद्रव्यापहारकम् ॥
भिन्नमन्त्रिबलं राजा पीड़येत् परिवेष्टयन्।
विग्रहः स च विज्ञेयोह्यन्यस्य कलहः स्मृतः ॥—Sukra, IV., vii., 251.

[2] Arthasastra, VII., 3.

and the character of the soldiers engaged in the armed conflicts.

"Blessed are the meek; for theirs is the kingdom of Heaven," says the Bible; "blessed are also they who wield the sword, for theirs is the Valhalla"[1]—that is the burden of the song of Prof. Cramb who vainly sought to establish friendly relations between Great Britain and Germany, "the two chosen people of God," just on the eve of the last great world war. A similar sentiment ruled the ideal of the warrior in ancient India. Retreat, to a Kshattriya, meant eternal shame whereas death in battle was the surest passport to heaven. Such were the prevailing sentiments of the warrior-class in ancient India. "Always exerting himself for the destruction of the robbers and the wicked people, a Kshattriya should put forward his prowess in battle...... Those among Kshattriya rulers who perform great sacrifices, who are possessed of a knowledge of the Vedas, and who gain victories in battle, become foremost of those who acquire many blessed regions hereafter by their merit. Persons conversant with the old scriptures do not applaud that Kshattriya who returns unwounded from battle. This has been declared to be the conduct of a wretched Kshattriya."[2] Thus did Bhisma discourse on the duties of a Kshattriya.

आहवेषु मिथोऽन्योन्यं जिघांसन्तोमहीक्षितः ।
युध्यमानाः परंशक्त्यास्वर्गं यान्त्यपराङ्मुखाः ॥[3]

"Those kings who seeking to slay each other in battle, fight with the utmost exertion and do not turn back, go to heaven" so said Manu. "A Kshattriya

[1] J. A. Cramb: England and Germany.
[2] Mahabharata, Santi-Raj, LX., 12-16.
[3] Manu, VII., 89.

should never cease from hostilities: his death in bed is a sin."[1]

"अधर्म्मः क्षत्रियस्यैष यच्छय्यामरणं भवेत्।"

"People should not regret the death of the brave man who is killed in battle. He is purged of all sins and for him is the kingdom of heaven. The fairies in the world above vie with each other for espousing the dead hero as their husband in the next life. Death in battle is therefore penance, virtue and eternal religion. Two persons in this world are entitled to go to heaven—the austere missionary and the man who is killed in battle." The exhortations of Sukracharyya to the military classes are so soul-stirring that they deserve to be quoted in full:—

आहवेषु मिथोऽन्योन्यं जिघांसन्तो महीक्षितः।
युद्ध्यमानाः परं शक्त्या स्वर्गं यान्त्यपराङ्मुखाः॥
आहवे निहतं शूरं नशोचेत कदाचन।
निर्मुक्तः सर्व्वपापेभ्यः पुतो याति सुलोकताम्॥
वराप्सरः सहस्राणि शूरमायोधने हतम्।
त्वरमाणाः प्रधावन्ति मम भर्त्ता भवेदिति॥

---

[1] Thus King Janaka, we learn from the Mahabharata, used to exhort his soldiers before battle:

योधानां दर्शयामास स्वर्गं नरकमेव च।
अभीतानामिमे लोका भास्वन्तो हन्त पश्यत॥
पूर्णा गन्धर्व्वकन्याभिः सर्व्वकामदुहोऽक्षयाः।
इमे पलायमानानां नरकाः प्रत्युपस्थिताः॥

Santi, XXIX., 3-4-5.

"Behold these are the regions endowed with great splendour for those that fight fearlessly. Full of Gandharba girls those regions are eternal and capable of granting every wish. There on the other side are the regions intended for those that fly away from battle! They would have to rot there for eternity in everlasting ingloriousness." The ideal of Sukracharyya is higher, because his fairies fight with each other for marrying the hero in the next life while the address of King Janaka resembles the addresses of the early Mahomedan Kaliphs and is echoed in the Quoran.

मुनिभिर्दीर्घतपसा प्राप्यते यत् पदं महत् ।
युद्धाभिमुखनिहतैः शूरैस्तद् द्रागवाप्यते ॥
एतत्तपश्च पुण्यञ्च धर्म्मश्चैव सनातनः ।
चत्वार आश्रमास्तस्य यो युद्धे न पलायते ॥
नहि शौर्य्यात् परं किञ्चित् त्रिषु लोकेषु विद्यते ।
शूरः सर्व्वं पालयति शूरे सर्व्वं प्रतिष्ठितम् ॥
चराणामचरा अन्नमदंष्ट्रा दंष्ट्रिणामपि ।
अपाणयः पाणिमतामन्नं शूरस्य कातराः ॥
द्वाविमौ पुरुषौ लोके सूर्य्यमण्डलभेदिनौ ।
परिव्राड् योगयुक्तो यो रणे चाभिमुखं हतः ॥

Sukra, IV., vii., 309-17.

A hard-hearted politician like Kautilya "almost oblivious of the great hereafter" also would divide heaven between the austere Brahmins (perhaps like himself!) and the great warriors of old.

यान्यज्ञसङ्घैस्तपसा च विप्राः
स्वर्गैषिणः पात्रचयैश्च यान्ति ।
क्षणेन तानप्यतियान्ति शूराः
प्राणान् सुयुद्धेषु परित्यजन्तः ॥

"Beyond those places where the Brahmins desirous of getting into heaven, attain together with their sacrificial instruments by performing a number of sacrifices, or by practising penance are the places which brave men losing life in good battles, are destined to attain immediately."

For such a warrior before whose eyes either the hues of heaven danced or the black of hell dangled there was absolutely no safety in retreat. "Hell yawns before him who flies in terror from a field of battle or who deserts either his ally or his master."

अपसरति यो युद्धाज्जीवितार्थी नराधमः ।
जीवन्नेव मृतः सोऽपि भुङ्क्ते राष्ट्रकृतं त्वघम् ॥

मित्रं वा स्वामिनं त्यक्त्वा निर्गच्छति रणाच्च यः ।
सोऽन्ते नरकमाप्नोति सजीवो निन्द्यतेऽखिलैः ॥[1]

Not only were the terrors of the life beyond the grave reserved for the cowardly deserter, but he had no place either in the family or society here below.[2] Such were the precepts which gave birth to the Rajput or the Maharatta people. Such was the Aryavarta which exhibited to the world a Rana Pratap or a Sivaji and for such a country was the memorable observation of Yuan Chwang made:

"Whenever a general is despatched on a warlike expedition although he is defeated and his country is destroyed, he is not himself subjected to bodily punishment, only he has to exchange his soldier's dress for that of a woman much to his shame and chagrin. So many times these men put themselves to death to avoid such disgrace."[3]

---

[1] Arthasastra, X., 3. This passage is admitted by Kantilya to be a quotation from the *Vedas*.

[2] Sukra, IV., vii., 328-329.

[3] IV., vii.

CHAPTER VIII

WAR : THE LAW RELATING TO ENEMY PERSONS AND ENEMY PROPERTY

"As to the practices in war in the ancient East," says Philipson, "it is on the whole a monotonous story of unrestrained cruelty, ferocity, barbaric treatment, and the entire disregard of all considerations save the attainment of the belligerent's object by whatever means possible." This statement of Philipson is perhaps partially true but he errs grievously when following Laurient he describes the code of Manu as, "*sans doute aussi, les loi de Manou respirent-un Machiavelisme profond.*" He admits, however, that the code of Manu established striking relaxations in the barbarous conduct of warfare but he seems to observe a great divergence between actual practice and idealistic theory and condemns the Hindus "beyond redemption." It will be the object of this chapter to prove conclusively that the ancient Indians entertained a very high ideal of warfare and their practice in general conformed to that noble ideal. On the contrary, the theory of all nations of antiquity besides India, was that declaration of war involved interruption of all relations between belligerents and conferred the right of unlimited violence upon them. The ethical superiority of international custom in ancient India is broadbased on six great moral principles, *viz.* :—

(*i*) The ancient Indians regarded war as a necessary evil to be taken recourse to (as shown in the last chapter) as a last expedient.

(*ii*) Certain well-defined rules guided all wars—rules which were sanctioned by religion and common humanity and were carried out by men ennobled by a sense of chivalry. The influence of chivalry upon the amelioration of warfare even in the middle ages in Europe has generally been acknowledged.

(*iii*) International usage in ancient India made a distinction between combatants and non-combatants and recognized the modern principle of various grades in enemy character.

(*iv*) The ancient Indians recognized war as a relation between states,[1] *e.g.*, the Agni Purana defines 'war' "as the direct result of injuries done to each other by two hostile monarchs," and the modern theory of the identity of the interests of the state with those of the individuals held good only in the case of a virtuous prince. Thus says Kamandaka :

धार्म्मिकस्याभियुक्तस्य सर्व्व एव हि युध्यते ।
प्रजानुरागधर्म्माभ्यां दुःखच्छेद्यो हि धार्म्मिकः ॥[2]

The same truth has been forcefully illustrated by Kautilya when he speaks about the various grounds of the defection of an entire people. "When a people are impoverished, they become greedy: when they are greedy, they become disaffected: when disaffected, they voluntarily go to the side of the enemy or destroy their own master."

क्षीणाः प्रकृतयो लोभं लुब्धा यान्ति विरागताम् ।
विरक्ता यान्त्यमित्रं वा भर्त्तारं घ्नन्ति वा स्वयं ॥

---

[1] *Cf.* Rousseau : "War then is not a relation of man to man but a relation of state to state, in which individuals are enemies only accidentally, not as men nor even as citizens, but as soldiers; not as members of the country, but as its defenders. Finally, each state can have for its enemies only rather states and not men, seeing that between things of a diverse character no true relation can be fixed."

J. J. Rousseau : Du Contrat Social, LI., iv.

Vattel's theory approaches Agni Purana's definition even more closely :

"It is against one sovereign that another makes war and not against the quiet subjects. The conqueror lays his hands on the possessions of the state, while private persons are permitted to retain theirs. They suffer but indirectly by the war; and to them the result is that they only change masters."

Vattel, Bk. III., ch. 9, § 167.

[2] Kam., IX., 44.

(*v*) *Dharma* did not recognize in ancient India, the institution of slavery. It has been repeatedly laid down both in the Dharmasastras as well as in the Arthasastras that an Aryya could never be reduced to slavery.

(*vi*) The dissociation of gods from party strifes mitigated the rigours of warfare in ancient India. All the other nations of antiquity, the Egyptians, the Assyrians, the Babylonians, the Jews, the Greeks and the Romans introduced gods as partisans into secular wars. The defeat of one state in ancient India did not necessarily involve the defeat and the suppression of the presiding deity of that state, while Babylonian history tells us that "after six hundred years Sutrakh-nakhante 'seized the hands of Bel.'" The bloody deeds of the Hebrews had likewise the implicit sanction of Divine vengeance. Virgil represents the gods in their anger overthrowing Troy. In Greece we hear of a conflict between Poseidon and Athena for the possession of Athens, between Poseidon and Helios as to Corinth and so on. In India, the nations struggled on for territorial aggrandisement, but the gods did not perhaps, except in the Vedic age, fight for the appropriation of various localities. In the Epics and the Puranas we have instances of gods fighting among themselves and very rarely with men, such as Arjuna fighting with Siva; but victory or defeat of states did not, in general, mean the victory or the defeat of the champion gods of the states. Thus religious rancour and religious fanaticism did not embitter secular warfare in ancient India for a very long time. These briefly are the causes which both *humanized* and *ennobled* warfare in ancient India.

Indian warfare stands in striking contrast to warfare throughout the world and in order to estimate the vastly liberal character of the wars in ancient India it is necessary to draw a picture of warfare not only in ancient but also in

comparatively modern times. Let us take up Egypt first. The description of the battle of Megiddo [1] and the newly discovered inscription of Ahmose [2] will serve our purpose: "The King himself, he led the way of his army, mighty at its head like a flame of fire, the King who wrought with his sword. He went forth none like him slaying the barbarians, smiting Retenu, bringing their princes as living captives, their chariots wrought with gold, bound to their horses [3]..
......Their champions lay stretched out like fishes on the ground. The victorious army of His Majesty went round counting the spoils, their portions.

"They brought in the booty which they had taken consisting of hands [severed from the slain], living prisoners, of horses and chariots, gold and silver."[4] Thutmoses III, the first great hero in the world according to Breasted, built a wall with human skulls and thus concluded his boast: "Lo! my majesty carried off the wives of that vanquished one together with his children, and the wives of the chiefs who were there together with their children.[5]

The monuments of Assyria and Babylonia as well as the records of the Hebrews bear witness to the barbarity of the Assyrians and certain of the Babylonian monarchs in warfare. The bodies of the slain were often mutilated, and rebel captives were impaled and subjected to the most horrible tortures. Those who escaped, were chained and enslaved. Whole nations were transplanted from one part of the empire to the other. The inscription of Assurnazirpal runs thus: "The nobles as many as had revolted, I flayed: with their skins I covered the Pyramid. Some

---

[1] Megiddo, fought by Thutmoses III in Asia Minor, 15th Century B.C.

[2] Ahmose, one of the officers of the Egyptian army of the Thutmosids.

[3] Breasted: Records, II., 413.

[4] *Ibid*, II., 616, 640.

[5] Breasted: II., 596.

of those I immured in the midst of the Pyramid; others I impaled above the Pyramid on stakes; others round about the Pyramid, I planted on stakes, many at the exit for my own country I flayed; with their skins I clad the fortress walls."[1]

The Persians did hardly mitigate the cruelties of war. Men, women and children were put to death or enslaved, and whole populations were transported. Mutilation of the dead and the torture of the living were freely exercised although there were some lighter shades to this picture.[2]

If we turn our eyes from early Orient, to early Occident we find Greek warfare characterized by great cruelty and severity. Hostilities in the Homeric times assumed the form of indiscriminate brigandage and extermination rather than subjection of the enemy was the usual practice. After Troy was taken, the Greeks did not think of taking possession of Priam's kingdom; the town was simply destroyed and the inhabitants were either enslaved or put to death. In historic times the conduct of the Greeks did not much improve although here and there our eyes meet with flashes of humanity. Athens, the "Schoolmistress of Hellas," brutally put to death all men of military age at Melos, and made slaves of the women and the children. The same story of indiscriminate slaughter and enslavement was told at Corcyra and at Mytiline.

The methods of Roman warfare were probably more humane than those of the Greeks, because life in Greece centred in the *polis* whereas a policy of absorption instead of extermination was forced upon Rome by the ceaseless march of events and yet such acts as the burning of crops, the demolition of houses, the carrying of men and

[1] Records of the Past, II., 134-277.

[2] *E.g.*, the treatment of Themistocles by Artaxares, *e.g.*, Cyrus's refusal to maltreat Greek embassies sent to him.

cattle as spoils were regarded as misfortunes to be borne rather than misdeeds to be complained of—"*esse enim quaedam belli jura, quae ut facere, ita pati sit fas; sata, exuri, derui, tecta, praedus hominum hecorumque agi, misera magis quam indigna patienti esse.*"[1] In the case of towns taken by assault, the leaders and occasionally all male defenders were put to the sword, and the women and children were all reduced to slavery.

Warfare in the middle ages took a hideous form. All considerations worthy of men and good Christians vanished. The following passage taken from a Christian historian, descriptive of the capture of Jerusalem (which was taken by storm in 1099), serves as an illustration of the unrestrained brutality of the crusaders :[2]

"No barbarian, no infidel, no Saracen, ever perpetrated such wanton and cold-blooded atrocities of cruelty as the wearers of the cross of Christ on the capture of that city. Murder was mercy, rape tenderness, simple plunder the mere assertion of a conqueror's right. Children were seized by their legs, some of them were plucked from their mother's breasts and dashed against the walls or whirled from battlements. Others were obliged to leap from the walls ; some tortured, roasted by slow fires. They ripped up prisoners to see if they had swallowed gold. Every one surprised in the temple was slaughtered till the reek from the dead body drove away the slayers. The Jews were buried alive in their synagogues."

The cruel practices of the Swiss and the Italian mercenaries in the middle ages struck terror into the heart of every law-abiding and peaceful citizen. Even the English armies were not free from ferocity. Thus Bernard gives a graphic account of the campaigns of Edward III in France :

"In the summer of 1346, an English army under Edward III landed on the coast of Normandy amongst a peaceful and industrious

---

[1] Livy : XXXI., 30.

[2] Milman : History of Latin Christianity, IV., 37.

people, who, says Froissart, had never heard a battle-cry, or seen an armed man. They took and sacked Barfleux and Cherbourg and marched on St. Lo.

"Fair and cheerful province, delicious sight to a hungry invader, with its hamlets and church towers, its substantial farms and large sleek cattle, thick orchards and green pastures, sweeping up hill and down dale to the winding margin of the sea! The English scattered themselves over it, and so advanced, burning and destroying—burning and destroying—over the rich flats of Beauvoisin to the suburbs of Paris. Immense booty was taken; yet the English host when it met the power of France at Crecy, was reduced to the utmost extremity of want."[1]

It is refreshing to turn one's eyes from this sickening tale of horrors in Europe to India which inspite of the condemnation of Philipson as "a country beyond redemption" carried on her wars in accordance with strict laws. Thus Bhisma[2] exhorted Judhisthir to be guided by righteous laws:

"A king should never desire to subjugate the Earth by unrighteous means even if such subjugation would make him the sovereign of the whole Earth. What king is there that would rejoice after obtaining victory by unfair means? A victory attained by unrighteousness is uncertain and never leads to heaven."

Bhisma elsewhere observes that a Kshattriya who destroys righteousness and transgresses all wholesome barriers does not deserve to be reckoned as a Kshattriya and "should be driven from society."

"नाधर्म्मेण महीं जेतुं लिप्सेत जगतीपतिः।
अधर्म्मविजयं लब्ध्वा को नु मन्येत भूमिपः॥
अधर्म्मयुक्तो विजयो ह्यध्रुवोऽस्वर्ग्य एव च।

* * * *

[1] Bernard: Growth of Laws and Usages of War, pp. 97-99.

[2] Mahabharata: Santi-Raj, XCVI., 1-3, 10.

यस्तुधर्म्मविलोपेन मर्य्यादाभेदनेन च ।
तां वृत्तिं नानुवर्त्तेत विजिगीषुर्महीपतिः ॥

"This has been declared to be the primeval law for warriors and from this law a Kshattriya should never depart when he strikes his foes in battle."

एषोऽनुपस्कृतः प्रोक्तोयोधधर्म्मः सनातनः ।
अस्माद्धर्म्मान्नच्यवेत क्षत्रियोघ्नन् रणे रिपून् ॥[1]

The theory of International Law by which the hardships of war have to a very large extent been modified is foreshadowed in the Mahabharata, where Bhisma counsels abstention from fruitless acts[2] of hostility, from insolence and from haughty speech and recommends humane treatment to the conquered people.

The victorious king should express sorrow at the death of the soldiers of the opposite party and try to conciliate the vanquished by kind treatment.

प्रहरिष्यन्प्रियं ब्रूयात् प्रहरन्नपि भारत ।
प्रहृत्य च प्रियं ब्रूयाच्छोचन्निव रुदन्निव ॥
नमे प्रिया ये स्म हताः संहृष्टाः परेऽपिच ।
नच कत्थनमेवाग्रमुच्यमानं पुनः पुनः ॥
अहो जीवितमाकाङ्क्षेन्नेदृशो वधमर्हति ।
सुदुर्लभाः सुपुरुषाः संग्रामेष्वपलायिनः ॥
कृतं ममाप्रियं तेन येनायं निहतोमृधे ।
इति वाचा वदन्हन्तॄन्पूजयेत रहोगतः ॥
हन्तॄणां च हतानां च पूजां कुर्य्यात् यथार्थतः ।
क्रोशेद्बाहुं प्रगृह्यापि चिकीर्षञ्जन संग्रहम् ॥[3]

---

[1] Manu, VII., 98.

[2] प्रियमेव वदेन्नित्यं नाप्रियं किञ्चिदाचरेत् ।—Santi, CIII., 10.

[3] Mahabharata, Santi, CII., 34-38. "Before smiting, O Bharata! and while smiting utter sweet words; after having smitten, show them compassion and let them understand that thou art grieving and weeping for them. Having vanquished an

'A king was not to kill a large number of troops of the foe although he should certainly do that which would make his victory decisive.'

"न सद्योऽरीन्विहन्याच्च द्रष्टव्यो विजयो ध्रुवः।"

This was probably too high an ideal set up before a conquering hero but even the writers of the Arthasastras[1] who were all worshippers in the shrine of Expediency and according to whom the end alone justified the means, counselled generous and chivalrous treatment of a conquered country.[2]

Thus, the Epics allow *Dharmajuddha* only, they do not permit *Kutajuddha*. It is only when we come to the study of the Arthasastras that we find them prescribing *Kutajuddha* under certain circumstances and with certain limitations. The Arthasastras looked upon war from two points of view: (*i*) from the point of utility, and (*ii*) from the point of "state necessity." Thus, according to Sukracharyya, a king should never destroy his army by recklessly undertaking wars—"न नाशयेत् स्वसेनान्तु सहसा युद्धकामुकः"[3] but being once in a quarrel the king was to behave himself in such a way "that the opposed might beware of him." Victory had to be obtained at any cost whether

army, the king should address the survivors saying—'I am not at all glad that so many have been slain by my troops! Alas, the latter though repeatedly dissuaded by me, have not obeyed my directions. I wish they (that are slain) were all alive! They do not deserve such death! They are all good men and true and unretreating in battle, such men indeed are rare! He that has slain such a hero in battle, has surely done that which is not agreeable to me!' Having uttered such speeches before the survivors of the vanquished foe the king should in secret honour those amongst his own troops that have bravely slain the foe. For soothing the wounded slayers for their sufferings at the hand of the foe, the king desirous of attaching them to himself should even weep seizing their hands affectionately."—P. C. Ray, Santi-Raj, p. 328.

[1] CIII., 19.

[2] *E.g.*, Sukra, IV., vii. (see later).

[3] Sukra, V., 7.

one followed the accepted rules of international usage or not. "धर्म्मयुद्धैः कूटयुद्धैर्हन्यादेव रिपुं सदा"[1] for, says Sukracharyya, it is folly to lose one's object[2] and therefore, a clever king should even suffer insult and humiliation at the outset to secure ultimate victory.

अपमानं पुरस्कृत्य मानं कृत्वा तु पृष्ठतः ।
स्वकार्य्यं साधयेत् प्राज्ञः कार्य्यध्वंसो हि मूर्खता ॥

But even Sukracharyya does neither deny the existence of Dharmajuddha, nor does he recommend Kutajuddha in every eventuality. The theory of state-interest triumphs over the inherent superiority of every ethical principle and he recommends कूटयुद्ध only for the weak.

There is no warfare, says he, which extirpates the *powerful*[3] *enemy* so much as कूटयुद्ध—"न युद्धं कूटसदृशं नाशनं बलवद्रिपोः" as one should follow the moral rules so long as one is powerful because people remain friends till then, just as the wind is the friend of the burning fire.

तावत्परो नीतिमान् स्याद्यावत् सुबलवान् स्वयम् ।
मित्रं तावच्च भवति पुष्टाग्नेः पवनो यथा ॥

The same principle has also been enunciated by Kautilya :[4]

"बलविशिष्ट कृतोपजापः प्रतिविहितकर्त्तुः स्वभूम्यां प्रकाशयुद्धमुपेयात् विपर्य्यये कूटयुद्धम् ।"

The overwhelming duty of self-preservation on the part of a state compelled it to take recourse to कूटयुद्ध but a small state before undertaking such wars was

---

[1] Sukra, IV., vii., 350.
[2] *Ibid*, IV., vii., 363.
[3] *Ibid*, IV., vii., 189.
Cf. also Agni, CCXL., 16.
[4] Arthasastra, X., 3

advised by Kautilya to enter into a subordinate alliance with a powerful state in the relationship of a sovereign and a client state.[1] It is only when outside help was not available that such a method of warfare was to be adopted. Thus says Manu :[2]

यदि तत्रापि संपश्येद्दोषं संश्रयकारितम् ।
सुयुद्धमेव तत्रापि निर्व्विशङ्कः समाचरेत् ॥

It is almost certain, however, that कूटयुद्ध formed the exception and not the rule as the distinction between combatants and non-combatants was firmly recognized by the ancient Hindus. Thus, though Sukracharyya[3] advocated a policy of "state-necessity," yet he recognized that Dharmajuddha allowed certain privileges both to combatants as well as to non-combatants.

न च हन्यात् स्थलारूढं नक्लीवं नकृताञ्जलिं ।
न मुक्तकेशमासीनं न तवास्मीति वादिनम् ॥
न सुप्तं न विसन्नाहं न नग्नं न निरायुधम् ।
नायुध्यमानं पश्यन्तं युध्यमानं परेण च ॥
पिवन्तं न च भुञ्जानमन्यकार्य्याकुलं न च ।
नभीतं नपरावृत्तं सतां धर्म्ममनुस्मरन् ॥
वृद्धो वालो न हन्तव्यो नैव स्त्री केवलो नृपः ।
यथायोग्यं तु संयोज्य निघ्नन् धर्म्मो न हीयते
धर्म्मयुद्धे तु कूटे वै न सन्ति नियमा अमी ॥

The Santiparva of the Mahabharata not only distinguishes between combatants and non-combatants but makes various gradations among combatants. Thus, "one that is walking unprepared in a road," *i.e.*, a mere traveller, or one engaged in drinking and eating, or one

---

[1] *Vide ante. Ibid*, VII., 15.

[2] Manu, VII., 176.

[3] Sukra, IV., vii., 355-58.

skilled in some special art, *i.e.*, persons admittedly following peaceful walks of life were granted immunities 'from being killed.'[1] Coupled with the general law, *viz.*, that an Aryya could not be reduced to slavery,[2-3] international usage or custom establishes the distinction between combatants and non-combatants. This distinction has been further emphasized by laws relating to what we now call "belligerent occupation" and "blockade," by land.[4] Even persons in the war zone who were mere onlookers could not be killed.[5] Messengers and Brahmans admittedly following their general peaceful lives were also not to be killed.[6]

The Mahabharata recognizes various grades in enemy character. Thus, according to the Mahabharata men who go out of the camp to procure forage or fodder, men who set up camps, and camp-followers as well as those who wait at the gates of the king or his ministers or those who do menial service to the army-chiefs, or those who are chiefs of such servants, shared the immunities of the non-combatants.[7]

---

1 Mahabharata: Santi-Raj, C., 27-29.

2-3 Vishnu, VI., 5, 151.
Manu, VIII., 412.
Arthasastra, III., 13.

4 See later.

5 Manu, VII., 92.

6 Gautama, X., 18.

7 Mahabharata: Santi-Raj, C., 27-29:

प्रसुप्तांस्तृषितान्श्रान्तान प्रकीर्णान्नाभिघातयेत् ।
मोक्षे प्रयाणे चलने पानभोजनकालयोः ॥
अतिक्षिप्तान्व्यतिक्षिप्तान्निहतान् प्रतनूकृतान् ।
अविस्रम्भान् कृतारम्भानुपन्यासात्प्रतापितान् ॥
बहिश्चरानुपन्यासान् कृतवेश्मानुसारिणः ।
पारम्पर्य्यागते द्वारि ये केचिदनुवर्त्तिनः ।
परिचर्य्यापरो द्वारी ये च केचन वल्गिनः ॥

Kautilya[1] the arch-apostle of expediency would permit emigration and immigration in times of war but Sukracharyya the ruthless advocate of the doctrine of state-necessity would extend enemy character to many persons enjoying immunity according to the Mahabharata.

From a passage in Kautilya's Arthasastra, it appears that belligerency did not put a stop to commercial intercourse, *ipso facto*, but if the king considered import of enemy's merchandise detrimental to the interests of his country then he could put a stop to such commercial intercourse :

तस्य प्रकृतयो दुर्भिक्षोपहता मामेष्यन्ति ; ....तं मे प्रकृतयो न गमिष्यन्ति ; विगृह्य चास्य धान्यपशुहिरण्यान्याहरिष्यामि ; स्वपण्योपघातीनि वा परपण्यानि निवर्त्तयिष्यामि ; परवणिक्पथाद्वा सारवन्ति मामेष्यन्ति.............इति परवृद्धिप्रतिघातार्थं प्रतापार्थं च विगृह्यासीत् ॥"[2]

The above conclusions are also confirmed by the evidence of foreigners. Thus says Megasthenes :

"Whereas among other nations, it is usual in contests of war, to ravage the soil, and then to reduce it to an uncultivated waste, among the Indians on the other hand *by whom husbandmen are regarded as a class that is sacred and inviolable*, the tillers of the soil even when battle is raging in their neighbourhood are undisturbed by any sense of danger, for the combatants on either side in waging the conflict make carnage of each other, but allow *those engaged in husbandry to remain quite unmolested*. Besides *they neither ravage an enemy's land with fire nor cut down its trees*."[3] The same thing has been repeated by Diodoros Sekulos :[4] "Among the

---

1 Arthasastra, VII., 1 : "परोपहतो वाऽस्य जनपदो मामागमिष्यति:"
Ibid.

2 *Ibid*, VII., 4.

3 Megasthenes, Frag. 1.

4 The Historical Library of Diodoros Sekulos, II., iii., 73.

ancient Hindus the armies on both sides slaughter one another, yet they never hurt the husbandman, as one who is a servant for their common good and advantage of them all; neither do they burn their enemies' country, or cut down their trees or plants." Thus Yuan Chwang also bears ample testimony to the humanity of Indian warfare—"Petty rivalries and wars are not unfrequent," says he, "but they do little harm to the country at large."[1]

Thus, the ancient Hindus clearly understood the modern international term, "enemy character." Kautilya was however obsessed with the idea of "*la gloire*" and he therefore extended the significance of "enemy character" even to such kings of the "Mandala or the circle of states, whose territories were contiguous to the dominions of the Vijigisu. Thus, Kautilya was guided by the "distance" theory of enmity, but he recognised also the enemy who created disturbances.

भूम्यन्तरं प्रकृतिमित्रः तुल्याभिजनः सहजः । विरुद्धो विरोधयिता वा कृत्रिमः ।[2]

भूम्येकान्तरं प्रकृतिमित्रं मातापितृसम्बन्धं सहजं ; धनजीवितहेतोराश्रितं कृत्रिममिति ।

Likewise friends were divided into (1) natural friends and (2) acquired friends.

Sukracharyya extended further the significance of enemy character. Gautama[3] recommended that persons who acted as messengers and those who declared themselves 'cows and Brahmans' should share the immunities of other combatants wounded or disabled, but Sukracharyya would not grant immunity to anybody who could bear arms. Thus, says he, "a Brahman does not incur sin

---

[1] Beal, Vol. II.

[2] Arthasastra, VI., 2.

[3] Gautama, X., 18.

even if he fights with arms and weapons in his hands and there is absolutely no sin in killing a man with a murderous intent." A Brahman who appeared with a murderous intent lost all the privileges of his caste. He became as good as a Sudra and the ordinary treatment of a belligerent was meted out to a Brahmana fighting obstinately with arms in his hands in a field of battle.[1]

आततायित्वमापन्नो ब्राह्मणः शूद्रवत् स्मृतः ।
नाततायिवधे दोषो हन्तुर्भवति कश्चन ॥
*　*　*　*　*　*
उद्यतेषुमथो दृष्ट्वा ब्राह्मणं क्षत्रबन्धुवत् ।
यो हन्यात् समरे क्रुद्धं युध्यन्तमपलायितम् ।
ब्रह्महत्या न तस्य स्यादिति धर्म्मेषु निश्चयः ॥

Even an infant could become tainted if it came upon a man with arms and it might with impunity be killed.

उद्यम्य शस्त्रमायान्तं भ्रुणमप्याततायिनम् ।
निहत्य भ्रूणहा न स्यादहत्वा भ्रूणहा भवेत् ॥ [2]

The ancient Hindus were not merely satisfied with laying down injunctions of religion for the

---

[1] Sukra, IV., vii., 325-28:

The Brahmans therefore formed a fighting caste as is also testified to by Kautilya although he does not put much faith in the invincibleness or the invulnerability of the Brahman army.

"ब्राह्मणक्षत्रियवैश्यशूद्रसैन्यानां तेजःप्राधान्यात् पूर्व्वं पूर्व्वं श्रेयः सन्नाहयितुम्" इत्याचार्य्याः। नेति कौटिल्यः—प्रणिपातेन ब्राह्मणबलं परोऽभिहारयेत् । प्रहरणविद्याविनीतं तु क्षत्रियबलं श्रेयः ; बहुलसारं वा वैश्यशूद्रबलमिति"—A. S., IX., 2.

Cf. also Sukra, IV., vii., 332-33:

सुदुष्टं सं यदा क्षत्रं नाशयेयुस्तु ब्राह्मणाः ।
युद्धं कृत्वापि शस्त्रास्त्रैर्न तदा पापभागिनः ॥
हीनं यदा क्षत्रकुलं नीचैर्लोकः प्रपीड्यते ।
तदापि ब्राह्मणा युद्धे नाशयेयुस्तु तान् द्रुतम् ॥

[2] Sukra, IV., vii., 326.

guidance of the army: nor was their consciousness for the sanctity of long-standing usage relied on, but elaborate rules were framed for keeping the soldiery strictly under control. Thus they were to be regularly inspected by the king[1] and properly officered.[2] The troops were to keep the arms, weapons and *uniforms* quite bright and ready for use.[3] They were held responsible for food, water and vessels in which food might be cooked.[4] They were subjected to daily parades[5] and arrangements were made for roll call[6] every morning and evening. All these salutary provisions increased the efficiency of the army and elaborate rules were laid down by which its treatment of the civilian population was vastly improved. Soldiers were liable to be punished by martial law if they criticised their commanders or if they maintained 'illicit connexion with evil-doers and enemies.'

स्वाधिकारिगणस्यापि ह्यपराधं दिशन्तु नः ।
मित्रभावेन वर्त्तध्वं स्वामिकृत्ये सदाखिलैः ॥[7]

असत्कर्त्राश्रितं सैन्यं नाशयेच्छत्रुयोगतः[7] Soldiers were required to forsake violence, rivalry, procrastination over state-duties, indifference to injuries of the king, conversation as well as friendship with enemies. They had to take a vow of enforcing the observance of these rules and they meted

---

[1] Arthasastra, I., 17 ; *cf.* also Kam., XV., 48.

[2] *Ibid*, II., 4. हस्त्यश्वरथपादातमनेकमुख्यमवस्थापयेत् । "Elephants, cavalry, chariots and infantry shall be officered with many chiefs."

[3] सुज्वलानि च रक्षन्तु शस्त्रास्त्रवसनानि च ।—Sukra, IV., vii., 385.

[4] अन्नं जलं प्रस्थमात्रं पात्रं वह्नन्नसाधकम् ॥

[5] सैनिकैरभ्यसेन्नित्यं व्यूहाद्यनुकृतिं नृपः ।—*Ibid.*

[6] सायं प्रातः सैनिकानां कुर्य्यात् संकलनं नृपः । जात्याकृतिवयोदेशग्रामवासान् विमृश्य च । कालं भृत्यवधिं देयं दत्तं भृत्यस्य लेखयेत् ॥

[7] *Ibid*, IV., vii., 391.

out death to those who violated them. (शासनादन्यथाचारान्[1] विनेष्यामि यमालयम्)

चण्डत्वमाततायित्वं राजकार्ये विलम्बनम् ।
अनिष्टोपेक्षणं राज्ञः स्वधर्मपरिवर्जनम् ।
त्यजन्तु सैनिकं नित्यं सल्लापमपि वा परैः ॥[2]

The ancient Indian kings did not follow the policy of war supporting the army and ample provision was made for paying off the salaries of the soldiers regularly. Thus full pay was to be granted to those who were trained soldiers and half pay was to be given to those who were under military training.

सैनिकाः शिक्षिता ये ये तेषु पूर्णा भृतिः स्मृता ।
व्यूहाभ्यासे नियुक्ता ये तेष्वर्द्धां भृतिमावहेत् ॥[3]

The soldiers were to give receipts in full satisfaction to the king in a form specifying wages.

कति दत्तं हि भृत्येभ्यो वेतनं पारितोषिकम् ।
तत्प्राप्तिपत्रं गृह्णीयाद्दद्याद्वेतनपत्रकम् ॥[4]

The troops were stationed near the village but outside it. Soldiers were required to make cash payments for articles bought and they were not allowed to enter the village without a royal "permit."

ग्रामाद्बहिः समीपेतु सैनिकान् धारयेत् सदा ।
ग्राम्य सैनिकयोर्न स्यादुत्तमर्णाधमर्णता ॥[5]

* * * * * *

नृपाज्ञया विना ग्रामं न विशेयुः कदाचन ।[6]

---

[1] Arthasastra, IV., vii., 386.
[2] *Ibid*, IV., vii., 382-83.
[3] Sukra, IV., vii., 390.
[4] *Ibid*, IV., vii., 389.
[5] *Ibid*, IV., vii., 379.
[6] *Ibid*, IV., vii., 383.

All these rules inculcated by the military codes of Indian antiquity remind us of the modern days of disciplined barrack life: all these rules taught the soldier to respect law and order and to be particularly dutiful towards innocent villagers; while a liberal scale of pay diminished their rapacity for pillage and booty. These rules did not have their permanent 'habitation' in military codes alone but were communicated to the soldiers evey eighth day ("संश्रावयेत् स्वनियमान् सैनिकानष्टमे दिने").[1]

It has been observed before, that the ancient Hindus understood the distinction between combatants and non-combatants fully well and laws of war gave various kinds of protection to combatants. Thus, it was one of the paramount duties of the soldiery to give QUARTER to enemy persons. Thus says the Mahabharata:

तेषां च भूमिं रक्षेयुर्भग्नान्नात्यनुसारयेत् ।
पुनरावर्त्तमानानां निराशानां च जीविते ॥
वेगः सुदुःसहो राजंस्तस्मान्नात्यनुसारयेत् ।
न हि प्रहर्त्तुमिच्छन्ति शूराः प्रद्रवतो भयात् ॥
"तस्मात्पलायमानानां कुर्य्यान्नात्यनुसारणम्"[2]

"The victor should protect the land newly conquered, from acts of aggression. He should not cause his troops to pursue too much the routed foe. The onset is irresistible of persons that rally after rout and that despairing of safety, assail their pursuers. For this reason,

---

[1] Sukra, IV., vii., 387.
[2] Mahabharata, Santi-Raj, XCIX., 12-14:

प्रसुप्तांस्तृषितान्श्रान्तान् प्रकीर्णान्नाभिघातयेत् ।
मोक्षे प्रयाणे चलने पानभोजनकालयोः ॥
अतिक्षिप्तान्व्यतिक्षिप्तान्विहतान् प्रतनूकृतान् ।
अविस्रब्धान्कृतारम्भानुपन्यासात्प्रतापितान् ।
बहिश्चरानुपन्यासान् कृतवेश्मानुसारिणः ।
पारम्पर्यागते द्वारि ये केचिदनुवर्त्तिनः ।
परिचर्यापरोद्वारी ये च केचन वल्गिनः ।

Santi-Raj, C., 27-30.

O King, thou shouldst not cause thy troops to pursue too much the routed foe. Warriors of courage do not wish to strike them that run away with speed."

Thus Bhisma urges two reasons contradictory in their very nature against the irresistible desire of a victorious army to extirpate its vanquished foe—the one is in accord with a sage counsel of military necessity, while the other is dictated by humanity.

So Bhisma lays down rules according to which *quarter* should be given to the following classes of persons:

"(1) those that are asleep;
(2) those that are thirsty or fatigued;
(3) those whose accoutrements have fallen away;
(4) those who have set their heart on final emancipation;
(5) those that are flying away;
(6) those that are walking along a road;
(7) those that are engaged in drinking and eating;
(8) those that are mad or insane;
(9) those that have been wounded mortally;
(10) those that have been exceedingly weakened by their wounds;
(11) those that are staying 'trustfully';
(12) those that have begun any work without being able to complete it (referring to sacrifices probably);
(13) those that are skilled in some special art;
(14) those that are in grief;
(15) those who go out of the camp for procuring forage or fodder;
(16) those who set up camps or who are camp followers; and lastly
(17) those who do menial services, and who are the chiefs of such servants."

It is clear from the above list that excepting persons wounded, camp followers, and 'those who have lost their coat of mail' all other persons are non-combatants.

Civilised warfare of modern times does not show the least quarter to some of these persons as well as to those who take to flight unless they actually surrender themselves. In the list of persons given by Manu to whom quarter should be shown as well as in the list furnished by Sukracharyya, quarter has been recommended to one who joins the palms of his hands in supplication, to one who flees with dishevelled hair and to one who sits down (as a sign of surrender) or to one who says, "I am thine."

........................न कृताञ्जलिं
न मुक्तकेशं नासीनं न तवास्मीति वादिनम् ।[1]

Sukracharyya, an exponent of the principle of expediency, recommended the extirpation of foes when beset with dangers and difficulties, when they are done up with hunger and thirst, when they are oppressed by disease,

---

[1] Manu, VII., 91-93.

न च हन्यात् स्थलारूढं न क्लीवं न कृताञ्जलिम् ।
न मुक्तकेशं नासीनं न तवास्मीति वादिनम् ॥
न सुप्तं न विसन्नाहं न नग्नं न निरायुधम् ।
नायुध्यमानं पश्यन्तं न परेण समागतम् ॥
नायुधव्यसनप्राप्तं नार्त्तं नातिपरीक्षितम् ।
न भीतं न परावृत्तं सतां धर्म्ममनुस्मरन् ॥

Cf. also Sukra, IV., vii., 354-59.

न च हन्यात् स्थलारूढं न क्लीवं न कृताञ्जलिम् ।
न मुक्तकेशमासीनं न तवास्मीति वादिनम् ॥
न सुप्तं न विसन्नाहं न नग्नं न निरायुधम् ।
नायुद्ध्यमानं पश्यन्तं युद्ध्यमानं परेण च ॥
पिबन्तं न च भुञ्जानमन्यकार्य्याकुलं न च ।
न भीतं न परावृत्तं सतां धर्म्ममनुस्मरन् ॥
वृद्धो बालो न हन्तव्योनैव स्त्री केवलो नृपः ।
यथायोग्यं तु संयोज्य निघ्नन् धर्म्मो न हीयते ।
धर्म्मयुद्धे तु कूटे वै न सन्ति नियमा अमी ॥

famine, or when they are asleep or engaged in taking food, etc., but he never denied quarter to persons who actually surrendered.[1]

It is evident from the passages quoted above, that the wounded were not killed nor were they left to die. From a passage in the Agni Purana we learn that one of the duties of infantry soldiers was to carry the dead and the wounded from the battlefield to a place of safety; the car-warriors, on the other hand helped to carry the wounded from a distance.[2]

Prisoners of war in ancient India were treated with humanity. Early custom gave the absolute right of life and death over the person of the vanquished. From a passage in Josephus we learn that Ptolemy Luthyrus overran the territory of Judea, strangled Jewish women and children, and boiled them in cauldrons, thus securing for his country a reputation for cannibalism.[3] Slavery was a mitigation to the lot of prisoners. Justinian's legal conscience was satisfied when he declared slavery a merciful relaxation of the strict rules of warfare which gave the victor a right over the lives of his captives.[4] An enlightened writer like Grotius [5] contented himself simply by advising Christians to remain satisfied with ransom. Even so late

---

[1] Sukra, IV., vii., 345:

दीर्घाध्वनि परिश्रान्तं क्षुत्पिपासाहितश्रमम् ।
व्याधिदूर्भिक्षकरकैः पीड़ितं दस्युविद्रुतम् ॥
पङ्कपांशुजलस्कन्नं व्यस्तं श्वासातुरं तथा ।
प्रसुप्तं भोजने व्यग्रमभूयिष्ठमसंस्थितम् ॥
घोराग्निभयवित्रस्तं वृष्टिवातसमाहतम् ।
एवमादिषु जातेषु व्यसनैश्च समाकुलम् ।
स्वसैन्यं साधु रक्षेत्तु परसैन्यं विनाशये ॥

[2] Agni, CCXXXVI., 44-48: Physicians and nurses took charge of the wounded. *Vide infra.*

[3] Josephus: Antiq., XII., 10; XIII., 6.

[4] Justinian: Inst., I., iii., 3.

[5] Grotius: III., vii., 9.

as the Treaty of Versailles, we find England and France entering into an agreement for the ransom of mutual prisoners.

In Greece the person of the defeated enemy was considered to be at the mercy of the conqueror. From a legal point of view, there was but little difference between a slave δουλος and a prisoner of war αιχμαλωτος. Humaner counsel however prevailed and we find constant protests against the sale of Hellenic prisoners of war to Hellenes in that period of criticism in Greece, *viz.*, the fourth century B.C. Thus Plato in his Republic strongly disapproves of the wanton destruction or enslavement of Hellenes to the people of the same race. In the *Heraclidae* of Euripides the struggle between custom and consciousness finds a tragic illustration when a prisoner was brought to Alemena and was told that he must suffer a miserable death, but objections were at once urged that such a practice would be contrary to the custom of the country:

ΑΓΓ ουκ εστ ανυστον τονδε σαι κατακτανειν.
ΑΛ αλλως αρ αυτον αιχμαλωτον ειλομεν.
εiργει δε δη τις τονδε μη θανειν νομος.
ΑΓΓ τοις τησδε χωρας προστατaισιν ου δοκει.
ΑΛ τι δη τοδ; εχθρους τοισιδ' ον καλον κατανειν.
ΑΓΓ ουχ οντιν αν γε ζωνθ' ελωσιν εν μαχη.

Grote bestows unstinted praise on Callicratidus, the Spartan Admiral because be declared that as long as he exercised the command no Greek would ever be reduced to slavery—εαυτον αρχοντος ουδενα Ελληνων εις το εκεινου δυνο τον ανδ ραποδισθηναι. King Aegislaus reminded his Spartan comrades that prisoners of war were men to be kept and not criminals to be punished: thus from out of this humane attitude sprang up the custom of ransom, mitigating the sufferings of those prisoners who could buy their liberty.

Roman treatment of prisoners was much milder than that of the 'refined' Hellenes. The Romans before they entered on a career of absorption and expansion resorted to the malpractices of the Greeks but later on they treated their prisoners well. After the fall of Carthagena, 209 B.C., Scipio allowed Mago and all the other free-born Carthaginian citizens to get back home. On several occasions Caesar liberated his prisoners on condition of their not taking up arms again. The institution of ransom was recognised and prisoners were liberated at times without ransom. Thus Pyrrhus followed the custom of releasing prisoners of war without ransom.[1]

The Indian treatment of prisoners was perhaps much more humane than that of the Greeks and of the Romans.

It was almost a settled custom that no Aryya should be reduced to slavery. Thus says Kautilya:

म्लेच्छानामदोषः प्रजां विक्रेतुमाधातुं वा ।[2]
न त्वेवार्यस्य दासभावः ॥

In the Vedic times, however, the Dasyus or the aborigines, if taken prisoners were reduced to slavery. Thus

---

Euri : Heraclid., 965 et ffg.

Mess.	Is it not possible for you to put him to death ?
Alc.	In vain then have we taken him prisoner.
	But what law hinders him from dying ?
Mess.	It seems not well to the chiefs of the land.
Alc.	What is this ? Not good to them to slay one's enemies ?
Mess.	No, any one they have taken alive in battle.

tr. Philipson.

[1] Nec mi aurum posco, nec mi pretium dederitis ;
Nec componantes bellum ; sed belligerantes,
....
Quorum virtuti belli fortuna pepercit,
Eorundem me libertati parcere certum est.

Cic : Deoffic, I., 12.

[2] Arthasastra, III., 13.

the word *Dasa* has the sense of 'slave' in several passages of the Rigveda :

> Not our own will betrayed us, but seduction,
> thoughtlessness, Varuna! Wine, dice, anger.
> The old is near to lead astray the younger:
> even slumber leadeth men to evil-doing.
> Slavelike may I, do service to the bounteous,
> serve free from sin, the good inclined to anger.
> This gentle lord gives wisdom to the simple:
> the wiser god leads on the wise to the riches.[1]

But neither in the epic era nor in subsequent times do we find any claims advanced on the part of the victors to reduce their captives to slavery. On the contrary, we have the positive testimony of the Agni Purana which enjoined upon monarchs the duty of abstaining from making captives of war. At any rate, if prisoners were made, they were to be set at liberty immediately on the conclusion of peace :

"A king should treat a prisoner of war ransomed and liberated as his own begotten son. A defeated army should not be fought again.. ....The wives of a defeated king do not pass to the victor[2] ....Of five means of appeasing the wrath of a stronger

---

[1] R. V., VII., 86, 7. *Cf.* also—

> Yadu and Turva, too, have been two Dasas, well disposed to serve
> Together with great store of kine.

Slavery in the Rigveda might be due to "wine, dice, gambling."—R. Y., X., 62, 10.

It is not the place here to trace the history of the institutien of slavery in ancient India. Kautilya's Arthasastra deals with rules relating to slaves and corveé. The slavery in ancient India as depicted by the Arthasastra differed from Roman slavery in three things, (*i*) the slaves in ancient India were not *Aryans* whereas at Rome, slaves were frequently, though not invariably, of Roman or at any rate of Italian origin, (*ii*) the Indian slave had not only the protection of religion but also the (*iii*) protection of law. Thus, violation of a female slave against her will led to punishment. Kautilya lays down general rules for masters in Chapter I, Book II, according to which those who did not treat their slaves (*dasas*), hired serfs (*Ahitakas*), and relatives well were to be taught their duty.

[2] Agni, CCXXXVI., 61-65.

adversary by gifts, the fifth one is setting at liberty prisoners captured in war."[1]

The humane treatment recommended by Kautilya and Sukracharyya to enemy person and enemy property in a country conquered or under belligerent occupation leaves no room for doubt that even if prisoners were made in ancient Indian warfare, they were very liberally treated and neither wholesale extirpation nor wholesale reduction to slavery was their lot; on the contrary they were rarely ransomed and frequently liberated.

Certain means of destroying combatants were also forbidden. This will be treated in the next Chapter.

With regard to enemy property, the evidence of the Greek writers[2] conclusively proves that wholesale destruction or ravaging of the enemy's property was not the general practice in ancient Indian warfare. The question of *booty* however raises some difficulty. It appears, however, that the king took a share of the booty in the Vedic age. The word *Udaja* with its variant *Niraja*[3] has been used to denote the share of the booty taken by the king after victory (संग्रामजिता). According to Manu Samhita, " chariots and horses, elephants, parasols, money, grain, cattle, women, all sorts of goods and valueless metals belong to him who takes them conquering (the possessor)." The Vedas enjoin upon the soldier 'who takes such booty, the duty of going into shares with the king and his comrades.'

रथाश्वं हस्तिनं छत्रं धनं धान्यं पशून्स्त्रियः ।
सर्व्वद्रव्याणि कुप्यञ्च यो यज्जयति तस्य तत् ॥
राज्ञश्चदद्युरुद्धारमित्येषा वैदिकीश्रुतिः ।
राज्ञाचसर्वयोधेभ्योदातव्यमपृथग्जितम् ॥[4]

---

[1] Agni, CCXL., 15-18.

[2] *Vide ante.*

[3] Maitrayani Samhita, for instance I., 10, 16; IV., 3, 1.

[4] Manu, VII., 96-97.

According to Sukracharyya, silver, gold and other kinds of booty belonged to him who won the same. The king was also to satisfy the troops by "giving them those things with pleasure according to the labour undergone":

रूप्यं हेम च कुप्यञ्च यो यज्जयति तस्य तत्।
दद्यात् कार्य्यानुरूपञ्च हृष्टो योधान् प्रकर्षयन्॥[1]

These two passages would lead to the conclusion that the soldiery were given up to unbridled plunder and the king was a sharer in that plunder. Probably the passage in Manu Samhita referred to the practice of the victors during the Vedic age, because it specifically referred to a passage in the Vedic literature according to which not merely gold and silver, *i.e.*, the personal belongings of soldiers slain on the battlefield, but also "money," "grain," "cattle," "women" would belong to the captor. Sukracharyya in the second passage quoted above, does not specifically refer to "money," "grain," "cattle" or "women" but goes further and observes that the king should protect the people of a conquered country like his own children and should realise "revenue" from a portion of the territory or the whole.

विजित्य च रिपूनेवं समादद्यात् करं तथा।
राज्यांशं वा सर्व्वराज्यं नन्दयीत ततः प्रजाः॥
*　　*　　*　　*
तत् प्रजाः पुत्रवत् सर्व्वाः पालयीतात्मसात्कृताः।[2]

This passage coupled with Kautilya's recommendations for the administration of a newly conquered territory[3] as well as the injunctions laid down by Bhisma[4] as relating to "the maidens captured from the enemy's

[1] Sukra, IV., vii., 372.
[2] *Ibid*, 373-74.
[3] Arthasastra.
[4] Santi-Raj., XCVI.

country, the wealth or the kine," lead us on to the inevitable conclusion that the system of taking booty was allowed although organised plunder was never permitted excepting perhaps in a *Kutajuddha* with the wild tribes of the forest named **अटवीबल** by Kautilya [1]:

तेषां कुप्यभृतममित्राटवीबलं विलोपभृतं वा कुर्यात् ।

Inhabitants of captured towns have at all times met with a sad fate. We need not go to the blood-curdling tales of the sack of Elam, the erasure of Babylonia and the destruction of Nineveh: Greece and Rome furnish us with many examples of inhumanity practised in ancient warfare. Thus, towns taken by storm in ancient Greece were liable to destruction—the men of military age were put to the sword, while the other citizens were reduced to slavery and general plunder followed. Roman practice was less barbarous but Polybius [2] held that the sacking of dwelling houses, the seizure of corn and other provisions, the setting fire to much property, the carrying off of the valuable dedicated arms of the porticoes and the destruction of the rest—all this was right and fair by the laws of war. The sack of Magdeburg in the Thirty Years' War rankled in the minds of men for a long time and demonstrated the necessity for International Law. Even so late as the year 1900, the murder of Blagoveschensk benumbed many a modern publicist.

Humanity in ancient India triumphed over the desire of revenge and according to Kautilya the territory of the conquered enemy should be kept so peacefully that all people might sleep without any fear : **कर्शनपूर्वं पर्यपासनं कर्म । जनपदं यथानिविष्टमभयं स्वापयेत् ।**[3] A great exponent of the

[1] Arthasastra, IX , 2.

[2] Polybius, V., 9.

[3] Arthasastra, 13, 4.

Cf. Liv., I., 38: Deditosque Collatinos ita accipio camque deditionis formulum esse : rex interrogavit "estisne vos legati oratoresque missi a populo conlatino, ut vos

principle of expediency like Kautilya not only counsels moderation but even urges kings not to use inflammatory and combustible powder when a fort can be captured by other means for, says he, "fire cannot be trusted; it not only offends gods, but also destroys the people, grains, cattle, gold, raw materials and the like." Then his utilitarianism rises up along with his humanity and he urges a further reason against reduction of forts by fire, etc.—"because the acquisition of a fort with its property all destroyed, is a source of further loss."

न त्वेव विद्यमाने पराक्रमेऽग्निमवसृजेत्। अविश्वास्योह्यग्निः दैवपीड़नंच ॥ अप्रतिसङ्ख्यातप्राणिधान्यपशुहिरण्यकुप्यद्रव्यक्षयकरः। क्षीणनिचयं चावाप्तमपि राज्यं क्षयायैव भवति ॥[1]

As in the cases of Greece and Rome, belligerent occupation in ancient India formed one of the means of acquiring property. War, according to Aristotle was a natural means of acquiring property—διο και η πολεμικη φυσεικ τητικη πω εσται......*Occupatio bellica*, similarly in the case of the Romans was for a very long time considered one of the modes of acquiring property. The same view was adopted also by Kautilya:

त्रिविधाश्च लम्भः—नवो, भूतपूर्व्वः, पित्र्य इति।[2]

The conqueror occupying an enemy's territory invariably followed the imperial policy of Rome so eloquently sung by Virgil in the following famous lines:—

Tu regere imperio populos, Romane, memento;
Hae tibi erunt artes, pacisque imponere morem,
Parcera subjectis, et debellare superbos.

---

populumque dederetis? "Sumus." "estne populus conlatinus in sua potestate? "est." deditsne vos populumque colatinum nrbem agros, aquam, terminos, delubra, ntensilia, divina humanaque omnia in meam populique Romani dicionem"? "dedimus" "at egio recipio."

[1] Arthasastra, XIII., 4.

[2] *Ibid*, XIII., 5.

The ancient Hindus recognised war as a necessary evil and as soon as the blasts of war had blown away and 'dovelike peace returned' a conqueror never failed to follow the principle of conciliation. Thus says the Mahabharata:[1] "if a hostile king be vanquished by the troops of the invader, the latter should not himself fight his vanquished foe. On the other hand, he should bring him to his palace, and persuade him to stay for a whole year—'I am thy slave'—whether he says or does not say this, the vanquished foe by living for a year in the house of his victor gains a new lease of life. If a king succeeds in bringing by force a maiden from the house of his vanquished foe, he should keep her for a year and ask her whether she would wed him or any one else. If she does not agree, she should then be sent back. He should behave similarly in respect of all other kinds of wealth that are acquired by force. The king should never appropriate the wealth confiscated from the thieves and others awaiting execution........... The kine taken from the enemy by force should be given away to the Brahmans. The bulls taken away from the enemy should be set to agricultural work or be sent to the enemy." According to Sukracharyya, the victorious king should first protect the people as his children, collect revenue from them, grant a portion of the revenue for the maintenance of the vanquished king and his family and he

[1] Mahabharata: Santi-Raj, XCVI., 3-6. Pratap Ray's translation.

वलेन विजितो यस्य न तं युध्येत भूमिपः।
संवत्सरं विप्रणयेत्तस्माज्जातः पुर्नभवेत् ॥
नार्वाक्संवत्सरात्कन्या प्रष्टव्या विक्रमाहृता।
एवमेव धनं सर्व्वं यच्चान्यत्सहसा हृतम् ॥
न तु वध्ये धनं तिष्ठेत् पिवेयुर्ब्राह्मणाः पयः।
युञ्जीरन्नप्यनड्वुहः चन्तव्यं वा पुनर्भवेत् ॥

Cf. also Agni, CCVXXVI., 22-28.

should then enjoy the remainder of the income.[1] The soldiery must remain outside the village and should not be permitted to enter the village without a royal permit and should on no account oppress the villagers.[2] Not simply that—military rule was not to be followed as Sukracharyya definitely lays it down that soldiers should not be appointed to any other work besides warfare "युद्धक्रियां विना सैन्यं योजयेन्नान्य कर्म्मणि" and villagers were not to come into daily contact with the soldiery.

Kautilya's Arthasastra throws a flood of light on the international consciousness of his age when he imposes the strictest injunctions upon a conquering hero not to covet the land, things and sons, or the wives of the king slain by him : on the contrary, he should re-instate in their own estates the relatives of the kings slain. The throne should also be preserved in the dynasty. If a king does not follow these precepts then he runs certain risk of exciting the displeasure of the 'circle of states' which is sure to rise up in arms against him. The passage of Kautilya is so full of wisdom and so "redolent of international odour" that it deserves to be quoted in full :

न च हतस्य भूमिद्रव्यपुत्रदारानभिमन्येत। कुल्यानप्यस्य स्वेषु पात्रेषु स्थापयेत्। कर्म्मणि मृतस्य पुत्रं राज्ये स्थापयेत्। एवमस्य दण्डोपनताः पुत्रपौत्राननुवर्त्तन्ते। यस्तूपनतान् हत्वा बध्वा वा भूमिद्रव्य-पुत्रदारानभिमन्येत, तस्योद्विग्नं मण्डलं अभावायोत्तिष्टते ये चास्यामात्याः।

---

[1] परराष्ट्रे हृते दद्यात् भृतिं भिन्नावधिं तथा। दद्यादर्द्धां तस्य पुत्रे स्त्रियै पादमितां किल।
हृतराज्यस्य पुत्रादौ सद्गुणे पादसम्मितम्। दद्याद्वा तद्राज्यतस्तु द्वात्रिंशांशं प्रकल्पयेत्॥
हृतराज्यस्य निचितं कोशं भोगार्थमाहरेत्॥
*   *   *   *   *   *

[2] नृपकार्य्यं विना कश्चिन्न ग्रामं सैनिको विशेत्।
तथा न पीड़येत् कुत्र कदापि ग्रामवासिनः॥
सैनिकैर्न व्यवहरेन्नित्यं ग्राम्य जनोऽपि वा।

Sukra, V., 84-85.

स्वभूमिष्वायुक्तास्ते चास्योद्विग्ना मण्डलमाश्रयन्ते। स्वयं राज्यं प्राणान् वा स्वाभिमन्यन्ते।[1]

स्वभूमिषु च राजानः तस्मात्साम्नाऽनुपालिताः।
भवन्त्यनुगुणा राज्ञः पुत्रपौत्रानुवर्त्तिनः॥

Actuated by motives of perpetuating dynastic rule, Kautilya, the moral prop of the vast Mauryya Empire, rises to a higher conception of imperialism in his chapter on लब्धप्रशमनम् and lays down rules of administration for a conqueror whose mission it should be to "subjugate the haughty," "to impose the custom of peace" and to lead nations on to a straightforward path of progress. Retain those customs of the vanquished which appear to you good, remove those which are bad, honour their language, customs and manners, reward the learned and the orators, heal the scars of war by releasing prisoners, and please your subjects by remission of taxes: tbis was the advice given to the Vijigisu by Kautilya—this was the policy followed by the Romans in framing their *pax Romana*; the same policy has also been consistently followed by the British in laying down the foundation-stone of the *pax Britannica*. Deviation from this policy of consolidation and conciliation after conquest spelt the ruin of the Roman Empire and will inevitably lead to the ruin of every empire of the present or of the future. Thus says Kautilya:

नवमवाप्य लम्भं परदोषान् स्वगुणैश्छादयेत्। गुणान् गुणद्वैगुण्येन स्वधर्मकर्मानुग्रहपरिहारदानमानकर्मभिश्च प्रकृतिप्रियहितान्यनुवर्त्तेत। यथासम्भाषितं च कृत्यपक्षमुपग्राहयेत्। भूयश्च कृतप्रवासम्। अविश्वास्यो हि विसंवादकः स्वेषां परेषां च भवति; प्रकृतिविरुद्धाचारश्च। तस्मात्समानशीलवेषभाषाचारतामुपगच्छेत्। देशदैवतसमाजोत्सवविहारेषु च भक्तिमनुवर्त्तेत। देशग्रामजातिसंघमुख्येषु चाभीक्ष्णं

[1] Arthasastra, VII., 16.

सत्रिणः परस्यापचारं दर्शयेयुः। माहाभाग्यं भक्तिं च तेषु स्वामिनः स्वामिसत्कारं च विद्यमानम्। उचितैश्चैनान् भोगपरिहाररक्षावेक्षणैः भुञ्जीत सर्वदेवताश्रमपूजनं च विद्यावाक्यधर्म्मशूरपुरुषाणां च भूमिद्रव्यदानपरिहारान् कारयेत्। सर्व्वबन्धनमोक्षणमनुग्रहं दीनानाथव्याधितानां च। चातुर्मास्येष्वर्धमासिकमघातं पौर्णमासीषु च चातुरात्रिकं; राजदेशनक्षत्रेष्वैकरात्रिकं; योनिबालवधं पुंसत्वोपघातं च प्रतिषेधयेत्। यच्च कोशदण्डोपघातिकमधर्म्मिष्टं वा चरित्रं मन्येत, तदपनीय धर्म्म्यव्यवहारं स्थापयेत्। चोरप्रकृतीनां म्लेच्छजातीनां च स्थानविपर्यासमनेकस्थं कारयेत्। दुर्गराष्ट्रदण्डमुख्यानां च परोपगृहीतानां च मन्त्रिपुरोहितादीनां परस्य प्रत्यन्तेष्वनेकस्थं वासं कारयेत्। अपकार समर्थाननुक्षियतो वा भर्तुविनाशमुपांशुदण्डेन प्रशमयेत्। स्वदेशीयान्वा परेण वाऽवरुद्धानपवाहित स्थानेषु स्थापयेत्। यश्च तत्कुलीनः प्रत्यादेयमादातुं शक्तः प्रत्यन्ताटवीस्थोवा प्रबाधितुमभिजातः; तस्मै विगुणां भूमिं प्रयच्छेत्; गुणवत्याश्चतुर्भागं वा। कोशदण्डदण्डदानमवस्थाप्य यदुपकुर्व्वाणः पौरजानपदान् कोपयेत्; कुपितैस्तैरेनं घातयेत्। प्रकृतिभिरुपकृष्टमपनयेत्। औपघातिके वा देशे निवेशयेदिति। भूतपूर्व्वे—येन दोषेणापवृत्तः, तं प्रकृतिदोषंछादयेत्। येन च गुणेनोपावृत्तः, तं तीव्रीकुर्य्यादिति।

पित्र्ये—पितृदोषांश्छादयेत्। गुणांश्च प्रकाशयेदिति।
चरित्रमकृतं धर्म्म्यं कृतं चान्यैः प्रवर्त्तयेत्।
प्रवर्त्तयेन्न चाधर्म्म्यं कृतं चान्यैर्निवर्त्तयेत्॥

A. S., XIV., i.

CHAPTER IX

THE AGENTS, INSTRUMENTS AND THE METHODS OF WARFARE

The agents employed by a state in ancient Indian warfare were twofold : (*i*) the armed forces of the state and (*ii*) the spies. Besides these, wild tribes were frequently employed either to fight the wild tribes similarly used by the enemy, or to harass the march and progress of the enemy in the rear. The armed forces of the state, it has been observed before,[1] were under strict military discipline. They carried arms openly,[2] and were under the orders of officers[3] and carried flags, ensigns[4] and wore distinctive uniforms.[5] According to Kautilya, for every ten members of each of the constituents of the army there must be one commander called *padika* ; ten *padikas* were placed under a *Senapati* and ten Senapatis were placed under the command of a *Nayaka*.

"अङ्गदशकस्यैक: पति: पदिक: ; पदिकदशकस्यैक: सेनापति:, तद्दशकस्यैको नायक इति" ।

The armed forces of a state were divided into various classes according (*i*) to the degree of trust that could be imposed on each constituent part, and (*ii*) secondly according to the vehicle used by each.

---

[1] *Vide supra.*

[2] "सर्व्वदेशकालशस्त्रवहनं"—A.S., X., 5.

[3] Arthasastra, X., 6.

[4] "स तुर्यघोषध्वजपताकाभि: व्यूहाङ्गनां संस्थापयेत्"—A. S., X., 6.

[5] Sukra, IV., vii.

Thus, Sukracharyya lays down the following Table :—

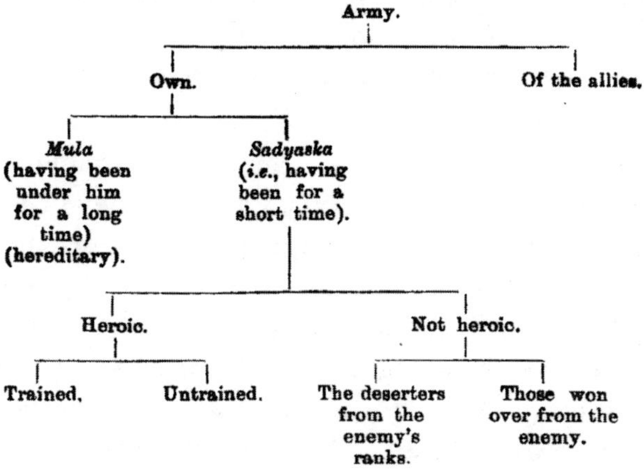

Kautilya describes the various kinds of army thus :—

(*i*) *Maula* hereditary army ; (*ii*) hired army ; (*iii*) *Sreni* army ; (*iv*) friend's army ; (*v*) the army composed of wild tribes (or अटवीबल). The exact time of recruiting and employing each kind of army has been clearly set forth by Kautilya, but that chapter luminous in the art of warfare does not interest us vitally at this point. It is difficult to understand what the Arthasastras mean by "श्रेणीबल." They are obviously a corporation of soldiers but is the corporation a corporation subject to the control of the state itself ? Or, does the corporation of soldiers form a band of condottieri as in the middle ages ? If the latter, then the passage[1] in Kautilya's Arthasastra which urges the employment of the *Srenibala* when the enemy is desirous of carrying on treacherous fight becomes inexplicable. And yet it is almost certain that there existed corporations also within the state.[2] Kautilya does not seem to look with much favour on the chief of such a corporation and he recommends the

[1] "मौलभृतश्रेणीमित्राटवीबलानामन्यतममलब्धदेशकालं "—A. S., VII., 8-9.

[2] "प्रभूतं मे श्रेणीबलं अक्षं मूलि यात्रायां व्यायातुम्" इति, "कस्य: प्रवास: श्रेणीबलप्राय: प्रतियोद्धा मन्त्रव्यायामाभ्याम् प्रतियोद्धुकामो दण्डबलव्यवहार:" इति श्रेणीबलकाल:—A. S., IX., 2.

adoption of various secret measures to discredit him in the estimation of his corporation and even to put an end to his life. Such an attitude of mind is only possible when the chief of a corporation ventures to become a sort of "*imperium in imperio*."

Sukracharyya's list does not contain the name of अटवीबल or wild tribes. They do not appear to have been amenable to the rules of International Law for they hankered after plunder and had to be rewarded by raw produce. तेषां कुप्यभूतमभित्राटवीबलं विलोपभृतं वा कूर्य्यात्.[1] They do not seem to have been regarded as "regulars" of an army, and they performed the functions of "guerilla troops" of the present times. They were engaged against wild tribes of a similar nature and for the purpose of harassing the rear of an enemy's army.

"मार्गदेशिकं परभूमियोग्यमरियुद्धप्रतिलोममटवीबलप्रायःशत्रुर्वा बिल्वं बिल्वेन हन्यतामल्पः प्रसारो हन्तव्यः" इत्यटवीबलकालः ।[2]

Armies were also divided according to the nature of the *vehicle* used for warfare. There were thus four kinds of armies : infantry, car warriors, cavalry and elephant men. Besides these regular forces, there were separate companies of men and animals who were entrusted with the duties of supplying weapons and ammunition to the fighting lines from the stores in the rear and of removing the wounded from the lines. These formed what we now call the 'labour corps.' Thus says Kautilya :

शिबिरमार्गसेतुकूपतीर्थशोधनकर्म्मयन्त्रायुधावरणोपकरणग्रासवहन मायोधनाञ्च प्रहरणावरणप्रतिविद्धापनयनमिति विष्टिकर्म्माणि ।[3]

"The examination of camps, roads, bridges, wells and rivers; carrying the machines, weapons, armours, instruments and provisions;

---

[1] *Cf.* also जानपदमेकार्थोपगतं तुल्यसङ्घर्षामर्षसिद्धिलाभं च श्रेणीबलं मित्रबलाच्च यः.........

[2] A. S., IX., 2.

[3] Arthasastra, X., 4.

carrying away the men that are knocked down, along with their weapons and armours—these constitute the work of free-labourers."

It has already been observed that specially humane treatment was accorded to the wounded. The army was generally followed by physicians and nurses. From a passage in Kautilya we learn, that some of these nurses were women :

"*Physicians with surgical instruments, machines, remedial oils* and cloth in their hands ; and *women with prepared food and beverage*, should stand behind, uttering encouraging words to fighting men" :

चिकित्सकाः शस्त्रयन्त्रागदस्नेहवस्त्रहस्ताः स्त्रियश्चान्नपानरक्षिण्यपुरु-षाणामुद्धर्षणीयाः पृष्ठतस्तिष्ठेयुः ।[1]

Thus, women-nurses alleviated the sufferings of the wounded and the dying at least two thousand years before Europe had organised her "Red-Cross" societies.

The army employed a very large number of spies. They were the "eyes and ears" of the king.[2] He was to look through their eyes, for says Kamandaka, "he that does not look through their eyes, stumbles down, out of ignorance, even on level grounds for he is said to be blind."

चारचक्षुर्नरेन्द्रः स्यात्सम्पतेत्तेन भूयसा ।
अनेनासम्पतन्मौढ्यात्पतत्यन्धः समेऽपि हि ॥[3]

They have been compared to the sun in energy and to the wind in movements, and the qualifications required of them were of an exacting character[4] : They must have been persons skilled in the interpretation of internal sentiments by conjecture and by external

[1] Arthasastra, X., 3.
[2] Kam., XII., 27.
[3] *Ibid*, XII., 30.
[4] *Ibid*, XII., 29.

gestures, accurate of memory, polite and soft in speech, agile in movements, capable of bearing up with all sorts of privations and difficulties, ready-witted, and expert in everything.

तर्केङ्गितज्ञः स्मृतिमान्मृदुर्लघुपरिक्रमः ।
क्लेशायाससहो दक्षचरः स्यात् प्रतिपत्तिमान् ॥[1]

As already observed, they had to serve their period of apprenticeship in an institute for espionage whose rules were very strict and which did not allow spies to know each other. Spies were employed not simply to gain information or to watch the movements of the enemy but also for the purposes of sowing dissension, for capturing the enemy's fort, country or camp with the aid of "weapons" "poison," or "fire," for [2] the purposes of most brutal assassinations of kings,[3] chiefs of the army, leading citizens, such as the councillors as well as for all purposes of devastation[4] and cutting off the supplies of the enemy. Espionage was not regarded with disfavour in ancient India and the ancient Hindus knew how to look sternly at facts and did not attempt to cloak their respect for humanity by elaborate rules like the civilized nations of the present times. The spies, however, in ancient India were regarded as ordinary 'combatants' and a short swift sentence of death was not generally passed on them. Their patriotism was recognised and nowhere is it laid down in the Dharmasastras or in the Arthasastras that a spy should be put to death instantaneously. An assassin or an arson of course deserved the extremest penalty allowed by law or imposed by necessity, but the spies as a class were not placed outside the pale of humanity.

[1] Kam., XII., 26.
[2] Arthasastra, XII., 1.
[3] *Ibid.*
[4] *Ibid*, XII., 4.

Instruments.

Weapons, according to Sukracharyya, were divided into two classes: *Astra* and *Sastra*. *Astra* is that which is thrown or cast down by means of charms, machines of fire. Astra is therefore, broadly speaking, of two kinds, charmed or tubular. Sastras are weapons by which cuts could be inflicted. It is not our present purpose to go into details about the large varieties of weapons used in ancient Indian warfare. International Law is concerned more with the prohibitions of the use of certain kinds of instruments in warfare rather than with their utility.

The Manusamhita[1] prohibits the use of certain kinds of instruments in warfare such as those which are *barbed*, poisoned or the points of which are blazing with fire:

न कूटैरायुधैर्हन्याद्युध्यमानोरणे रिपून् ।
न कर्णिभिर्नापिदिग्धैर्नाग्निज्वलिततेजनैः ॥

Let us take up the question of poisoned arrows first. Poisoned arrows were used in early stages of civilisation in almost every country. Thus, when Odysseus had gone to Ephyra to procure a deadly drug for smearing his arrows, Ilus refused to give it to him, on the ground that the gods would not sanction such an act:

φα'ρμακον ανδροφο'νον διζημενος "οφρα οι' 'ε'ιη
ιο'υς χ'ριεσθαι χαλκ'ηρεας 'αλλ'ο με'ν ο'υ' ο'ι
δωκεν, επει ρ'α θεο'υς νεμεσιζετο αιεν εοντας[2]

Poisoned arrows were certainly used during the Vedic times. Thus, in a hymn of the Rigveda two distinct kinds of arrows are referred to: the one is poisoned (or *alakta*) and has a head of horn (*rur-sirsni*); the other is copper,

---

[1] Manu, VII., 90.

[2] Odysseus, I., 261-3.

bronze or iron headed (भयोमुखं). Poisoned (दिग्ध) arrows are also mentioned in the Atharvaveda. Thus says the Rigveda:[1]

> Now to the shaft with venom smeared, tipped with deer-horn, with iron mouth,
>
> Celestial, of Parjanya's seed, be this great adoration paid.
>
> Loosed from the bowstring fly away, thou arrow, sharpened by our prayer,
>
> Go to the foemen, strike them home, and let not one be left alive.

And Atharvaveda:

> From the tip have I exorcised the poison, from the anointing and from the feather socket; from the barb (*spastha*), the neck, the horn, have I exorcised the poison.
>
> Sapless, O arrow! is thy tip; likewise thy poison is sapless; also thy bow of a sapless tree, O sapless one! is sapless.
>
> They who mashed, who smeared, who hurled, who let loose—they all made impotent; impotent is made the poison mountain.[2]

And again,

> Like an arrow, smeared, O Lord of men, like an adder, O Lord of cattle—that arrow of the Brahman is terrible; with it he pierces the insulting.[3]

Long before the time when Manu's Code was reduced to writing however, the advance of humanitarianism led to the disuse of poisoned arrows. No grounds of humanity could possibly be urged against arrows blazing with fire unless it were superstition or ignorance (which similarly condemned the use of the fatal 'cross bow' during mediæval times), and therefore their use continued. Thus, in an obstinate siege-warfare, fire-arrows were recommended by Kautilya with one great limitation, *viz.*, that "when a fort could be captured by other means, no attempt

---

[1] R. V., VI., 75, 15-16, Griffith.

[2] A. V., IV., 6, 7, Whitney.

[3] A. V., V., 18, 15, Whitney. See also V., 31, 4.

should be made to set fire to it." A kind of stick painted with inflammable mixture and wound round with a bark made of hemp, zinc and lead was called a "fire arrow." तेन (by inflammable powder) अवलिप्त: शणत्रपुसीसवल्कवेष्टितो बाण इत्याग्नियोग:[1] These arrows were not *generally* used in wars. Evidence of this fact is deducible from the list of the weapons given by Kautilya, to be kept in charge of the Superintendent of the royal armoury.[2] These weapons were probably generally made use of although the possibility for the use of certain delusive and destructive contrivances as mentioned by Kautilya in his chapter on siege warfare, had not been lost sight of and the Superintendent of armoury was advised to stock these latter kinds of weapons along with all new inventions of workmen :

ऐन्द्रजालिकमौपनिषदिकं च कर्म्म कर्म्मान्तानां च ।[3]

The range of arrows in those days must have been very limited and military necessity must have taxed the ingenuity of skilled workmen to find out a device by which persons and things at a distance could be struck. In the list of weapons mentioned by Kautilya *Sarvatobhadra* and *Jamadagnya* have been mentioned—the one was according to the commentator a cart with wheels and capable of rapid revolution; when rotated, it threw stones in all directions. It resembled the "catarpillar" invented by the Assyrian experts of old. *Jamadagnya* was another contrivance for shooting arrows.

It is not the place here to discuss whether the ancient Hindus knew the gunpowder and the gun although the vital interest attached to the subject perhaps requires a passing mention. It has however been one of the articles of faith in military circles, that Europe owes its knowledge

---

[1] Arthasastra, XIII., 4.

[2] *Ibid*, II., 18.

[3] *Ibid*, II., 18.

of gunpowder to the Saracens, a knowledge which dealt the death-blow to chivalry and ushered in a revolution in warfare, specially in siege warfare. We have several passages in Sukranitisara which clearly prove that the ancient Hindus knew the use of guns. Thus says Sukracharyya:

"People expert in military instruments know of diverse agencies named *astras* and *sastras*, varying according to short or large size and the nature and mode of the sharp edges. The *nalika astra*[1] is known to be of two kinds according to size, large or small. The short or small *nalika* is the cylindrical instrument to be used by infantry and cavalry and having an oblique and straight hole at the origin, the length of five *vitastis* or two cubits and a half, a sharp point both at the forefront and at the origin, which can be used in marking the objective, which has fire produced by the pressure of a machine, contains stone and powder at the origin, has a good handle at the top, has an inside hole of the breadth of the middle finger, holds gunpowder in the interior and has a strong rod. The instrument strikes distant objects according as the bamboo or bark is thick and hollow and the balls are long and wide. The large *nalika* is that which has a post or wedge at the origin or breech, and according to its movements, can be pointed towards the aim, has a wooden frame and is drawn on carriages: if well used, it leads to victory."[2]

---

[1] नालिकं द्विविधं ज्ञेयं बृहत् क्षुद्रविभेदतः ॥
तिर्य्यगूर्द्ध्वच्छिद्रमूलं नालं पञ्चवितस्तिकम् ।
मूलाग्रयोर्लक्ष्यभेदितिलविन्दुयुतम् सदा ॥
यन्त्राघाताग्निकृद्ग्रावचूर्णधृक्कर्णमूलकम् ।
सुकाष्ठोपाङ्गबुध्नञ्च मध्याङ्गुलविलान्तरम् ।
स्वान्तेऽग्निचूर्णसन्धातृशलाकासंयुतं दृढम् ।
लघुनालिकमप्येतत् प्रधार्य्यं पत्तिसादिभिः ॥
यथा यथा तु त्वक्सारं यथा स्थूलविलान्तरम् ।
यथा दीर्घं बृहद्गोलं दूरभेदि तथा तथा ॥
मूलकीलभ्रमाल्लक्ष्यसमसन्धानभाजि यत् ।
बृहन्नालिकसंज्ञं तत् काष्ठबुध्नविनिर्मितम् ।
प्रवाह्यं शकटाद्यैस्तु सुयुक्तं विजयप्रदम् ॥
सुवर्चिलवणात् पञ्चपलानि गन्धकात् पलम् ।
अन्तर्धूमविपक्वार्कस्नुह्याद्यङ्गारतः पलम् ॥
शुद्धात् संग्राह्य सञ्चूर्ण्य सम्मील्य प्रपुटेद्रसैः ।
स्नुह्यर्काणां रसोनस्य शोषयेदातपेन च ।
पिष्ट्वा शर्करवच्चैतदग्निचूर्णं भवेत् खलु ॥
सुवर्चिलवणाद्भागाः षड्वा चत्वार एव वा ।
नालास्त्रार्थाग्निचूर्णे तु गन्धाङ्गारौ तु पूर्ववत् ॥
* * * * * *
अङ्गारस्यैव गन्धस्य सुवर्चिलवणस्य च ।
शिलाया हरितालस्य तथा सीसमलस्य च ॥
हिङ्गुलस्य तथा कान्तरजसः कर्पूरस्य च ।
जतोर्नील्याश्च सरलनिर्य्यासस्य तथैव च ॥

[2] Sarkar's translation.

Thus evidently the passage quoted here, points to the inevitable conclusion that the author of these lines at any rate knew the gun (the rifle) and the cannon. These weapons, continues the author, may be made of iron or of some other metal and must be kept clean. He also gives a composition of gunpowder : "Five *palas* of Suvarchi salt, one *pala* of sulphur, one *pala* of charcoal from the wood of *arka*, *snuhi* and other trees burnt in a manner that prevents the escape of smoke, *e.g.*, in a closed vessel, have to be purified, powdered, and mixed together, then dissolved in the juices of *snuhi*, *arka* and garlic, then dried up by heat and finally powdered like sugar. The substance is called gunpowder." "Experts," continues the author, "make gunpowders in various ways and of white and other colours according to the relative quantities of the constituents :—charcoal, sulphur, *subarchi*, stones, *harital*, lead, *hingul*, iron filings, camphor, *jatu*, indigo, juice of *sarala* tree, etc." These passages have been regarded as subsequent interpolations. The mention of नालिक occurs only in the passages mentioned above. Sukracharyya does not however, repeat his ideas about "नालिक" in his book. The whole conception of the gun, the cannon and the gunpowder is so very modern, contend the advocates of the 'interpolation theory,' that it could not possibly have found a place in a text book on Nitisastra at such an early date as that of Sukracharyya. Dr. Ray has proved, however, the indigenous origin of Hindu alchemy and it is also in evidence that *saltpetre* was mentioned by Charaka and Susruta. From this it cannot be argued of course, that the Hindus of Sukra's date possessed a competent knowledge of guns and gunpowder.

Kautilya's Arthasastra, however, gives us valuable hints on the point. In his chapter on "siege-warfare," he gives directions for the preparation of various kinds of inflammable powders. Thus, small balls prepared from the mixture of *Sarala devadaru* (tree), *putitrina* or stinking grass, *guggulu, sriveshtaka* (turpentine), the juice of *sarja* and lac combined with dungs of an ass, camel, sheep and goat are inflammable.

सरलदेवदारुपूतितृणगुग्गुलुश्रीवेष्टकसर्ज्जरसलाक्षागुल्विकाः खरोष्ट्र-जीवानां लण्डं चाग्निधारणम् ।[1]

The mixture of the powder of *prijla*, the charcoal of *avalguja*, wax and the dung of a horse, camel and cow is an inflammable powder to be hurled against the enemy.[2]

प्रियालचूर्णमवल्गुजमषिमधूच्छिष्टमश्वखरोष्ट्रगोलण्डमित्येव क्षेप्योऽग्नि-योगः ।

Inflammable powders could be used against a besieged enemy by various contrivances. Thus, they could be tied to the tails of various kinds of birds such as the vulture, crow, parrot, *maina*, pigeon, etc., and they could be set at large towards the forts. This could be done only when the besieging army was almost at the very gates of the fort. If the camp of the besieging army, however, was at a distance, then archers from an elevated place might aim "fire arrows" at the fort and thus set fire to it. Now the question naturally arises, how could the balls mentioned above be used? Animals could not very well carry them, neither could they be hurled against an enemy from a distance. Some contrivance therefore, must have existed for the effective use of balls against the fort of the enemy. Was that contrivance the नालिक of Sukracharyya? It is difficult to answer the question from the Arthasastra of Kautilya unless we make bold to identify the 'fire arrow'

---

[1] Arthasastra, XIII, 4.

[2] *Ibid.*

with a wooden rifle.[1] It is almost certain however, that the mechanical composition given by Kautilya of a second kind of inflammable powder is almost identical with the composition of the second variety of gunpowder mentioned by Sukracharyya. Thus says Kautilya :

"सर्व्वलौहचुर्णमग्निवर्णं वा कुम्भीसीसत्रपुचूर्णं वा पारिभद्रकपलाश-पुष्पकेशमषीतैलमधुच्छिष्टकश्रीवेष्टकयुक्तोऽग्नियोगः । [2]

So, the ingredients were (*i*) the powder of all the metals as red as fire, (*ii*) the mixture of the powder of *kumbhi*, (*iii*) lead, (*iv*) *trapu* (zinc), mixed with charcoal powder of the flowers of (*v*) *paribhadraka* (deodar), (*vi*) *palása* and (*vii*) hair and with oil, wax and turpentine. It will be seen that powdered metals, lead and zinc as well as charcoal powder mixed up with the other substances produce a kind of inflammable powder.

The recipe of Sukracharyya for preparing gunpowder is as follows: (*i*) charcoal, (*ii*) sulphur, (*iii*) *suvarchi*, (*iv*) stones, (*v*) *harital*, (*vi*) lead, (*vii*) *hingul*, (*viii*) iron filings, (*ix*) camphor, (*x*) *jatu*, (*xi*) indigo, (*xii*) juice of Sarala tree,[3] etc. It will be seen, therefore, that the constituent elements of gunpowder in both Kautilya's Arthasastra and Sukranitisara agree. Even if the passages in Sukranitisara be regarded as interpolations, the passages in the Arthasastra cannot be regarded as "literary fraud" and therefore, the inevitable conclusion is that the ancient Hindus knew the composition of gunpowder and actually used it, in whatsoever rudimentary a form it might be, at least fifteen hundred years before the Saracens introduced it to Christian Europe.

---

[1] तेनावलिप्त. शणत्रपुसीस वल्कवेष्टितो बाणइत्याग्नियोगः ।—A. S. XIII. 4.

[2] *Ibid.*

[3] *Cf.* also the Mahabharata, Santi, LXIX. 45 : "He should plant on the ramparts of his forts *Sataghnis* and other weapons."

As observed before, these inflammable powders were regarded as इन्द्रजाल and were very sparingly used. Bombardments of besieged towns according to ancient practice were very common but even Kautilya recognized the fact that when a fort could be captured by other means, no attempt should be made to set fire to it. As remarked before, the reasons assigned by Kautilya do credit both to the head as well as the heart of the great exponent of ancient Hindu diplomacy :

नत्वेव विद्यमाने पराक्रमेऽग्निमवसृजेत्। अविश्वास्योह्यग्निः दैवपीड़नं च। अप्रतिसङ्ख्यातप्राणिधान्यपशुहिरण्यकुप्यद्रव्यक्षयकरः। क्षीणनिचयं चावाप्तमपि राज्यं क्षयायैव भवति।[1]

Kautilya's Arthasastra conclusively proves also that the ancient Hindus knew very well the composition of many kinds of asphyxiating gases but not even Kautilya advocates their indiscriminate use even in the most stubborn siege-warfare :

"The smoke caused by burning the powder of *putikita* (a stinking insect), fish, *katutumbi* (a kind of bitter gourd), the bark of *satakardama* (a kind of tree) or the powder of *putikita*, *kshudrala* (the resin of the plant) and *hemavidari*; the smoke caused by burning the leaves of *putikaranja*, yellow arsenic, realgar, the seeds of *ganja*, the chaff of the seeds of red cotton *asphota*, *khacha* and the dung and urine of a cow causes blindness.[2] Similarly, the roots of *kali*, *kushtha*, *nada*, *satavari*, or the powder of a snake, the tail of a peacock *krikana*, and *panchkushtha* together with the chaff causes smoke and thereby destroys the eyes of all animals."[3] Similarly, there

---

[1] A. S., XIII., 4.

[2] Arthasastra, XIII., 4.

[3] *Ibid*, XIV., 1:

पुतिकीटमत्स्यकटुतुम्बीशतकर्दमेध्मेन्द्रगोपचूर्णं पुतिकीटक्षुद्रालाहेमविदारीचूर्णंवा बस्तशृङ्गखुरचूर्णंयुक्तमन्धीकरो धूमः।—A. S., XIV., 1.

were gases which could cause instantaneous death. All these asphyxiating gases and shells, if used, would have rendered the theatre of war a veritable hell. They were perhaps very rarely used, if ever: and antidotes were known against these hellish devices. Thus a man could render his eyes secure not by masks but by the application of ointments and of medicinal "water-burns." The opening lines of Bk. XIV, however, lead one to the belief that the secret methods of injuring an enemy were used not collectively in warfare but rather individually against certain persons by *Mlechchhas* and such other spies who could assume the disguises of idiots, dumb, deaf and blind persons, etc. Fortunately for civilisation it was difficult to conceive of an army of 'miserable mortals' and therefore, it is quite probable that the institution of four castes, the humanity of the people, the momentum of tradition would revolt against the indiscriminate use of such Machiavellian tactics in warfare.

चातुर्वर्ण्यरक्षार्थमौपनिषदिकमधर्म्मिष्ठेषु प्रयुञ्जीत। कालकूटादिः विषवर्गः श्रद्धेयदेशवेषशिल्पभाजनापदेशैः कुब्जवामनकिरातमूकवधिरजडान्धच्छद्मभिः म्लेच्छजातीयैरभिप्रेतैः स्त्रीभिः पुंभिश्च परशरीरोपभोगेष्वाधातव्यः॥

As regards the methods of warfare, the difference between *Dharmajuddha* and *Kutajuddha* has been pointed out before. A धर्म्मयुद्ध stood for honourable fight guided by all the laws of chivalry. In *Dharmajuddha*, declaration followed commencement of hostilities and the king showed the trust-character of his office, by exhorting his soldiers

पुतिकरञ्जपत्रहरितालमनःशिलागुञ्जारक्तकार्पासपलालान्यास्फोटकाचगोशकृद्रसपिष्टमन्धीकरो धूमः॥

See also pp. 409-410, Arthasastra, Mysore Ed. It is difficult to identify the constituent elements, but these chapters in Kautilya's Arthasastra testify to the great advance that some people, at any rate, in ancient India made in the science of alchemy.

just on the eve of the battle thus : " I am a paid servant like yourselves ; this country is to be enjoyed together with you ; you have to strike the enemy specified by me."[1] The कूटयुद्ध on the other hand, resembled the "heraldless and truceless wars " among the Greeks ηθλεμος ακηρυκτος και ασπονδος and actual operations began with the commencement of hostilities : पूर्व्वं च प्रहरणकाला: कूटयुद्धहेतव:. Political expediency dictated the adoption of this form of warfare in all cases by a king " when he did not possess a strong army, when he did not succeed in his intrigues or when he could not secure a position favourable to himself." It was then that the grim doctrine of "state necessity " applied :

" बलविशिष्ट: कृतोपजाप: प्रतिविहितकर्त्तु: स्वभूम्यां प्रकाशयुद्ध-मुपेयात् विपर्य्ययेकूटयुद्धं "[2]

The methods chiefly employed in a कूटयुद्ध could be classified under, (*i*) Devastation, (*ii*) Stratagems, (*iii*) Assassination, (*iv*) Poison. All these methods received their sanction from political expediency and not from international or interstatal morality.

Devastation in a limited form has been sanctioned by International Law at all times according to the military exigencies of the army. Thus, according to Grotius,[3] only such ravage is tolerable as in a short time compels the enemy to seek peace and even this restriction on the theory of unlimited destruction was hedged round by further limitations. Vattel [4] authorised unlimited destruction of a hostile territory in two cases, firstly, against the onrush of a nation of barbarians and, secondly, when the

---

[1] Arthasastra, X., 3. सं'ग्रामस्तु निर्द्दिष्टदेशकालो धर्म्मिष्ट: सं'हत्य दण्डं ब्रूयात्— "तुल्यवेतनोऽस्मि ; भवद्भि: सह भोग्यमिदं राज्यं ; मयाऽभिहित; परोऽभिहन्तव्य: ।"

[2] Arthasastra, X., 2.

[3] Grotius, III., 12.

[4] Vattel : III., §167-68.

need " for making a barrier for covering a frontier against an enemy who could not be stopped in any other way," was imperative. The Hague Regulations allow destruction of enemy's property only when " such destruction is imperatively demanded by the necessities of war." The same theory with regard to devastation was held in ancient India. Thus says the Mahabharata : " A king should (on the approach of the enemy) set the inhabitants of the woods on the highroads (these are the अटवीबल), and if necessary, cause whole villages to be removed, transplanting all the inhabitants to minor towns or the outskirts of great cities............He should himself withdraw all stores of grain. If that becomes impossible, he should destroy them completely by fire. He should set men for destroying the crops on the field of the enemy. Failing to do this, he should destroy these crops by means of his own troops. He should destroy all the bridges over the rivers in his kingdom. He should bale out the waters of all the tanks in his dominions, or if incapable of baling them out, cause them to be poisoned ....He should destroy all the smaller forts of his kingdom. He should also cut down all the smaller trees excepting those called Chaitya. He should cause the branches of all the larger trees to be lopped off, but he should not touch the very leaves of those called Chaitya."[1] Kautilya in his Arthasastra recommends the devastation of the enemy's country through the help of wild tribes,[2] and if the enemy aided by his friend shut himself up in an impregnable fort, then his neighbouring enemies might be employed to lay waste his territory.[3]

---

[1] Mahabharata : Santi-Raj, LXIX., 35 et ffg. tr. Pratapchandra Ray.

[2] A. S., XII., 1.

[3] Arthasastra, XIII., 3 :

मित्रेणाश्रितश्चेच्छत्रुरयाशो स्थातुमिच्छेत्, सामन्तादिभिः मूलमस्य हारयेत् ; दण्डेन वा घातुमिच्छेत्। तमस्य घातयेत् तौ चेन्न भिद्येयाताम् प्रकाशमेवान्योन्यस्य भूम्यां पणेत ॥

Conquerors, according to Kautilya are of three kinds, (*i*) a just conqueror, (*ii*) a demon-like conqueror, and (*iii*) a greedy conqueror. The just conqueror remains satisfied with mere obeisance. The greedy conqueror hankers after gain in the shape of dominions or of wealth. The demon-like conqueror satisfies himself not merely by seizing the land, treasure, sons and wives of the conquered, but by taking the very life of the conquered himself.[1] Stratagems as ruses practised on the enemy were frequently resorted to specially in the मन्त्रयुद्ध or the 'battle of intrigues' proving the truth of the general maxim that war is a conflict of wits as much as it is a conflict of arms. Such stratagems were generally practised by तीक्ष्ण spies but they did not extend to the breach of sacred obligations such as would correspond, for instance, to the violation of flags of truce in modern times.

Assassinations for public purposes by spies were regarded with approval in ancient as well as in mediæval times. Grotius justified such assassinations if carried out *bonâ fide.* Kautilya recommended cold-blooded murder of kings, chiefs of the army, chiefs of corporations and other councillors. These assassinations were however committed by spies who were liable to the extremest penalty of law when actually caught. Wholesale poisoning was frequently resorted to. As already pointed out, the use of poisoned arrows or the practice of poisoning of wells was not approved. The Mahabharata prohibited the poisoning of wells and tanks and "suspicion in respect of the seven branches of administration."[2]

---

[1] एषोऽभियोक्तारो धर्मासुरलोभविजयिन इति। तेषामभ्यवपत्त्या धर्मविजयी तुष्यति।...... परेषामपि भयात् भूमिद्रव्यहरणेन लोभविजयी तुष्यति............भूमिद्रव्यपुत्रदारप्राणहरणेन असुरविजयी ॥—A. S., XII., 1.

[2] Mahabharata : Santi-Raj, CIII., 10. From another passage of the Santiparva, LXIX, it would appear however, that poisoning of tanks was one of the means of

Poisoning of individuals or the cattle of the enemy was however not prohibited by the Arthasastras. Thus spies under concealment might capture the enemy's fort, country or camp with the aid of weapons, poison, or fire.[1] Kautilya's Arthasastra lays down elaborate rules for the administration of poison by spies with almost matchless precision and cold-bloodedness. Thus, spies residing in enemy's country as traders could sell poisoned liquors to soldiers.[2] Spies under the garb of servants might sell poisoned grass and water and thus kill the enemy's cattle, horses and elephants.[3] Prostitute-spies might entice away young princes, chiefs of corporations or of the army, who frequently paid the wages of their sin in the shape of ignominious death. Spies under the disguise of cooks could mix poison with food and thereby cause death. All these counsels are perhaps counsels of perfection in black art, because, no state would permit the universal administration of poison within its territory by the spies of its enemy; and yet a publicist is astounded by the liberal treatment accorded to the spies by kings in ancient India. They were not branded as a class, nor were they put to death the moment they were recognised Thus states on the eve of a war swarmed with spies and Bhisma[4] advised the expulsion of beggars, cartmen, eunuchs, lunatics and maimed persons so that they might not be employed for such nefarious purposes. In places of public resort, in *tirthas*, in assemblies and in the

devastation. Such contamination of water does not seem to be prohibited even by the Hague conferences. Such contaminations took place both during the Boer War as well as during the recent European War. See General Maurice's book on the Boer War.

[1] A. S., XII., 1.

[2-3] A. S., XII., 4.

[4] Mahabharata: Santi-Raj, LXIX., 49-51.

20

houses of the citizens the king set on foot competent spies.[1] Thus was attempted a partial check on the weird activities of a disciplined system of universal espionage in ancient India.

[1] *Cf.* Arthasastra, XIV., 1.

Cf. also Arthasastra, XIII., 1.

चातुर्वर्ण्यरक्षार्थमौपनिषदिकमधर्मिष्ठेषु प्रयुञ्जीत । कालकूटादिः विषवर्गः श्रद्धेयदेशवेषशिल्पभाजनापदेशैः कुब्जवामनकिरातमूकबधिरजडान्धच्छद्मभिः म्लेच्छजातीयैरभिप्रेतैः स्त्रीभिः पुंभिश्च परशरीरोपभोगेष्ववधातव्यः ॥—A. S., XIV., 1.

CHAPTER X

NEUTRALITY

There is an almost universal consensus of opinion among publicists that nations in antiquity had no clear cut ideas about Neutrality. "Since in antiquity, there was no notion of an International Law, it is not to be expected that neutrality as a legal institution should have existed among the nations of old. Neutrality did not exist even in practice, for the belligerents never recognised an attitude of impartiality on the part of other states.[1]" One of the grounds for this mistaken notion is that in antiquity as well as in mediæval times there was a total absence of a proper vocabulary of neutrality. The Romans spoke of neutrality as *medii, amici* or *pacati*. Grotius devoted very little attention to neutrality. He established only two rules relating to neutrality in the chapter entitled *De his, qui in bello medii sunt*. The first rule related to the justice or injustice of the causes of the belligerents and neutrals were advised not to help a belligerent whose cause was unjust. The second rule again dealt with distributive justice or equality of treatment towards both the belligerents. Bynkershoek does not use the term neutrality but calls "neutrals" '*non-hostes*' and describes them as belonging to no party. In the seventeenth century, "the terms neutral and neutrality occur in a Latin and a German dress as well as in English, but they had to be adopted into the French language before their use became general." Vattel writing in 1758, spoke of *neutre* and *neutralite*.

---

[1] Oppenheim: International Law, II., 347.

Modern researches have, however, led to discoveries which might almost discredit the theory of publicists like Oppenheim. Thus, in Greece the terms commonly used to express neutrality were ησυχιαν αγειν, ησυχαζειν (to keep quiet), μηδετερος μηδετερος (to be of neither party) and οιδια μεσον, εκτου μεσου καθησθαι (the party occupying an intermediate position). These words, of course, merely imply abstention from hostilities but do not imply the positive and the negative aspects of neutrality. The doctrine of neutrality did not find a congenial soil in the all-absorbing ambition of Rome. Her customary attitude was expressed by one phrase "either for or against"; no intermediary position was conceded or even admitted. Thus says Livy [1]—"*media......nulla via est......Romanos aut socios aut hostes habeatis oportet.*"

In ancient India *Asana* or neutrality formed one of the six forms of state policy. *Vatavyadhi* declared that peace and war were the only two forms of state policy: Kautilya, however, voted in favour of the six and defined neutrality as उपेक्षणमासनं [2] or indifference. In the Kautilyan circle of states the two kings who did not identify themselves with the विजिगीषु or the अरि or their client states, were the मध्यम king and the उदासीन king. The word मध्यम occurs in one passage of the Rigveda [3] and in another passage of the Atharvaveda. [4] There is a difference of opinion among scholars as to the meaning of the word but the most accepted interpretation is that of an "arbitrator," although the

---

[1] Livy, XXXII., 21.

[2] Arthasastra, VII., 1.

[3] R. V., X., 97, 12.

[4] A. V, IV., 9, 4. "Of whomsoever, O ointment, thou creepest over limb after limb, joint after joint, from thence thou drivest away the *yaksma* like a formidable *madhyamaci.*" Roth assigns the meaning *intercessor* to *madhyamaci*; Zimmer accepts it in the sense of a 'mediator.' Whitney considers this meaning "implausible" and suggests "midmostman." *Cf.* also Kam., VIII., 16, and Manu, VII., 158.

definition of a Madhyama king in Kautilya would lead one to agree with Geldner in translating मध्यम as a "neutral" king. Thus Kautilya defines a मध्यम king as one occupying territory close to both the Vijigiṣu and his immediate enemy in front and who is capable of helping both of them, or resisting either of them individually.

अरिविजिगीष्वोर्भूम्यनन्तरः संहतासंहतयोरनुग्रहसमर्थो निग्रहे चासंहतयोर्मध्यमः ।[1]

A Madhyama king is the head of a sovereign state having under its control 'the client states.'[2] A उदासीन king on the other hand, is one whose dominions lie beyond the territories of the other kings of the circle of states and who is very powerful, capable of helping the sovereign states such as those under the *Vijigisu*, the *Ari* and the *Madhyama* king "either taken together or individually, or of resisting any of them individually."

अरिविजिगीषुमध्यानां बहिः प्रकृतिभ्यो बलवत्तरः संहतासंहतानामरिविजिगीषुमध्यमानामनुग्रहे समर्थो निग्रहे चासंहतानामुदासीनः ।[3]

Thus, from the definition of the मध्यम and उदासीन it will be seen that the ancient Indian conception of neutrality made a nearer approach to the mediæval conception of neutrality of Grotius and Rachel rather than the developed ideas of neutral attitude in modern times but it is not true to say that the ancient Indians did not understand an attitude of neutrality at all. If we trace the development of the idea of neutrality in mediæval times in Europe we shall be in a position to understand the Hindu idea of neutrality. According to Grotius' views neutral states were bound to abstain from active participation in the hostilities

[1] A. S., VI., 2.

[2] *Vide supra.*

[3] A. S., VII., 2.

between the belligerents. The idea was also abroad in the middle ages of Europe that a neutral state must be either weak or mean-spirited. The same views seem to have been held by Kautilya "न मां परो नाहं परमुपहन्तुं शक्तः" इत्यासीत् ।[1] But this was not all. Self-interest guided the ancient Hindu theory of neutrality. Neutrality according to the same author should be observed by a king when he considered himself equal to his enemy in prowess, or when he thought that his interests would be served better by observing neutrality rather than by taking part in actual hostilities.

यदि वामन्येत—"न मे शक्तः परं कर्म्माण्युपहन्तुं ; नाहं तस्य कर्म्मोपघातोवा ; व्यसनमस्य श्ववराहयोरिव कलहे वा स्वकर्म्म-मनुष्ठानपरो वा वर्द्धिष्ये" इत्यासनेन वृद्धिमातिष्ठेत् ॥

Thus the idea seems to have been entertained that realization of self-interest, sometimes at any rate, demanded the observance of neutrality: this was a substantial step in advance in the growth and development of the idea of neutrality. Thus says Kautilya once more:

सन्धिविग्रहयोश्चेत् परकर्षनात्मोपचयं वा नाभिपश्येत्, ज्यायानप्यासीत् ॥[2]

According to ancient Hindu ideas, neutrality was of three kinds: (*i*) *sthana* keeping quiet; *asana* (withdrawal from hostilities) and *upekshana* (negligence). Keeping quiet, after maintaining a particular kind of policy is *sthana*; withdrawal from hostile actions for the sake of one's own interests is *asana*; and taking no steps against an enemy is *upekshana*.

स्थानमासनमुपेक्षणं चेत्यासनपर्यायाः । विशेषस्तु गुणैकदेशे स्थानं ; स्ववृद्धिप्राप्त्यर्थं आसनमासनं ; अपायानामप्रयोगः उपेक्षणमिति.[3]

---

[1] Arthasastra, VII., 1.

[2] *Ibid*, VII., 3.

[3] A. S., VII., 4.

Thus according to the classification made above, *sthana* and *upekshana* would be the two forms of neutrality corresponding to "neutrality" of the present times.

Neutrality, according to Kautilya, might be preserved even after the declaration of war[1] under certain exceptional circumstances. A study of the Arthasastra would lead us to the belief that observance or non-observance of neutrality at any particular juncture was dictated by considerations of state-interest or national policy, rather than by the promptings of moral or juridical consciousness. This view gains support from the desperate attempts made by the *Vijigisu* and the *Ari* in the 'circle of states' to catch hold of a neutral king and from a passage in Kautilya's Arthasastra it would appear that a Madhyama king was regarded with great disfavour by a Vijigisu.[2]

"मध्यमं त्वरिविजिगीष्वोर्लिप्समानयोर्मध्यमस्य पार्ष्णिं गृह्णतो: लब्धलाभावगमने यो मध्यमं मित्राद्वियोजयति, अमित्रं च मित्रमाप्नोति, सोऽतिसन्धत्ते। सन्धेयश्च ह्यनुरूपकुर्व्वाणो न मित्रं मित्रभावादुत्क्रान्तम्॥

The theory of "enmity by distance" propounded by Kautilya makes a *Madhyama's* position almost unbearable but the theory of the balance of power conclusively proves that neutrality in ancient Indian polity was to a large extent prompted by juridical consciousness.

मण्डलं वा प्रोत्साहयेत्—"अतिप्रवृद्धोऽयं मध्यमः सर्व्वेषां नो विनाशाय अभ्युत्थितः सम्भूयास्य यात्रां विहनाम" इति।[3]

Thus, if the Madhyama king attempted to overthrow the balance of power within the circle of states then the Vijigisu could incite the whole circle against him. From

---

[1] *Vide* VII., 4.

[2] A. S., VII., 13.

[3] A. S., VII., 10.

the dawn of civilisation, neutrality has stood in the way of unbridled conquest unless the conqueror could by disregard of all laws or rules of morality convert the neutral into either a friend or a foe. A conquering king was advised by Kautilya to seek the protection of the *Madhyama* king and the *Udasina* king when they were both esteemed by the circle of states.

A Madhyama king is neutral like the *Udasina*, but the former is on the point of joining the fray while the latter through negligence—as the name signifies it—or through state-interest is desirous of maintaining a neutral attitude.

A ruthless conqueror panting for a world-empire like an Alexander, a Caesar, a Louis XIV, a Napoleon or a Wilhelm would not stop when the 'way is long and the gate is narrow,' or when rules of International Law stand in his way. They are all cast aside and the conqueror marches on with ceaseless fury. It was for such a conqueror that Kautilya wrote his Arthasastra and with a cold cynicism unparalleled for boldness he recommended "a conqueror first to seize the territory of the enemy close to his country, then that of the *Madhyama* king"; "this being taken, he should seize the territory of the neutral king. This is the first way to conquer the world."[1]

एवं विजिगीषुरमित्रभूमिं लब्ध्वा मध्यमं लिप्सेत्। तस्मिन्नुदासीनम्।
एष प्रथमो मार्गः पृथिवीं जेतुम् ॥

Such then in brief, are the ancient Hindu ideas of neutrality. These ideas were much more developed than those of the classical Greeks and the Romans and even those of the European nations before the French Revolution. The elaborate rules regarding neutrality framed by

---

[1] Arthasastra, XIII., 4.

modern International Law are the triumph of the last two centuries. Inspite of these rules the last great war clearly demonstrated once more the truth of the remark that weak states cannot maintain an attitude of neutrality in a great world-conflict. Violations of neutrality were very frequent during the last war. Thus was Belgium violated; so was Chinese territory violated; so did Chili protest against the violation of her neutrality before the naval battle off Valpariso; so was Greece compelled to espouse the cause of the *Entente*. The ancient Indians did not frame elaborate rules for intercourse between neutral states and belligerents partly because they lived thousands of years before the triumph of modern civilisation and to a very large extent because, war with them did not absolutely put an end to all intercourse even between the belligerent states. Trade and commerce went on almost uninterrupted [1] and therefore we do not meet with elaborate discussions in the Arthasastras about the rights and obligations of neutral powers.

---

[1] *Vide ante*. *Cf.* also

यस्य वा स्वदेशादन्यदेशाद्वा पण्यानि पण्यागारतया गच्छेयुः तान्यस्य "यातव्याल्लब्धानि" इति सत्रिणश्चारयेयुः बहुलीभूते शासनमभिव्यक्तेन प्रेषयेत्—"एतत्ते पण्यं पण्यागारं वा मया ते प्रेषितं; सामवायिकेषु विक्रमस्व, अपगच्छ वा ततः पणशेषमवाप्स्यसि" इति। ततः सत्रिणः परेषु ग्राहयेयुः—"एतदरिप्रदत्तम्" इति॥ शत्रुप्रख्यातं वा पण्यमविज्ञातं विजिगीषुं गच्छेत्। तदस्य वैदेहकव्यञ्जनाः शत्रुमुख्येषु विक्रीणीरन् ततः सत्रिणः परेषु ग्राहयेयुः—"एतत्पण्यमरिप्रदत्तम्" इति।

A. S., IX., 6.